Stan Vines

A Sense of No Direction

Limited Special Edition. No. 20 of 25 paperbacks

To Ruth
Thanks for your Help.

About the Author

After spending the recent 20 years in Greece in shipping, Middle East and Africa business and sailing the islands and the previous 20 in London involved in computing, Marketing and publicity, and manufacturing and property development Stan Vines decided to return and spend some time in his home village in the UK. Although having been there for periods on visits, part of this mission was to get to know his family better after such a time away. At the same time, he would be prompted to continue writing a book he started as a recreation some two years before. Austin Macauley showed interest in its publication and in the summer of 2018, the book was completed on a visit to Greece and the finished manuscript sent to them. He has now started two further books to form a trilogy spanning the last 45 years of ups and downs, cataloguing his life and experiences.

To family and friends and Skipper

Stan Vines

A SENSE OF NO DIRECTION

AUSTIN MACAULEY PUBLISHERS™

LONDON · CAMBRIDGE · NEW YORK · SHARJAH

A CIP catalogue record for this title is available from the British Library.

ISBN 9781528923620 (Paperback)
ISBN 9781528964272 (ePub e-book)

www.austinmacauley.com

First Published (2019)
Austin Macauley Publishers Ltd
25 Canada Square
Canary Wharf
London
E14 5LQ

"If you can dream and not make dreams your master
If you can think and not make thoughts your aim
If you can meet with triumph and disaster
And treat those two imposters just the same."

If – Rudyard Kipling

Contents

Preface

No matter where you are or what you are in life, there is always somewhere or something else that you could be doing, always something else going on. Some people can think about it and do nothing more and are happy, but some regret not doing the things they imagine. Others take the bull by the horns and get up and go and do those somethings. Ultimately, it doesn't matter what you do as long as you are happy and enjoy it and don't cause harm to others.

I started writing because one night, in a port in Greece on my boat, there was a terrible storm. Skipper, my pointer dog of nearly 17 years who unfortunately passed away last year, and I were being thrown about by the wind and waves and this was in the port; the storm was so severe. The internet in the office on the quay went down as did my 4G connection. I was bored and anxious and Skipper, for all his experience on the water, was terrified. I remembered different times of anxiety from many years ago and started to write what is now the introduction. It triggered a chain reaction of many more recollections and a third of the book was born. Nothing happened for two years until back in the UK a nurse in the local surgery giving me a flu jab said that she was bored. I said that I had just spent 20 years in Greece, hence the check-ups and jabs. She said she wished that she had done something similar. To spur her on and to show that it doesn't take so much to pick up and travel (the downside is never so down), I say, "Well, if you think that is a big thing to do, when we were kids, a friend and I went to Australia. I am writing a book about it." She asked me to send her a copy of what I'd written so far and I did. My sister asked to see it, being a bit of a literary buff, said she enjoyed the first few chapters and maybe it is worth finishing and try to have it published? She provided encouragement throughout the finishing to the last chapter. Others, Gillian, a rather special and very dear wordsmith I had the privilege to meet and spend some time with along the way, also James McBride, author of 'Aircrew Stories' provided encouragement. His "Everyone has a book in them", although blearily, fanned the flame during inebriated evenings reminiscing in island ports of Greece on sailing trips. Chris, my travel companion and major character in the story, didn't know about the book until it was done. He wholeheartedly approves, the story wouldn't be the same without him.

Here it is. I hope that you enjoy it, I enjoyed writing it and it's all true. I hope too that it may inspire others to take the chance and find situations and do things that create wholesome memories that later can be related to friends and company to bring some joy and that same essence of fun into the world; it needs it, continually. We wanted to meet different people and to see their cultures and at the same time give the world a taste of what can come from a small village in Lancashire. We think we did.

Introduction

What had we got ourselves into?

In a bed of sorts in a darkened room after travelling thousands of miles it was the lowest time, and the first time I felt deeply insecure. Outside the doorway of the room, there was a glimmer of an electric light without a shade in the distance down the hallway. No glass in the room window, just cracked and torn polythene sheets fastened with tape.

Well, at least we were one floor up so there was little chance of anyone coming through there as Chris had commented a few minutes earlier. It was -1°C when we arrived that afternoon, now in the middle of the night, goodness knows what the temperature was, just stark and very, very cold. The suede fur lined jacket I had bought was a godsend now. It was cheap and part of a plan as we knew it would be colder where we were heading. It looked more expensive than it was, and the worry was that maybe I would end up fighting with someone who might have wanted to take it. I remember thinking maybe that time was now.

We had travelled the five km or so by airline bus (if that's what you would call it, something more like a wreck from a scrap yard) from the airport to the city centre gathering our thoughts on what to do next. People milling around looked at us as they passed, no friendly or welcoming glances at all. The general mood appeared to be that most people were just concerned about something. Nothing specific or apparent, they just looked worried. All men, there was not a woman in sight. Everything and everybody was in very poor appearance relative to our European standards. We had seen much similar before, but here it was different. They were not so much ragged and worn but cobbled together in dress and looking desperate. The city was raw, primitive and wild; I remember for a while feeling even more desperate than they looked. All that stuff about being from a part of the British Commonwealth and being safe as we were English and respected just didn't come to mind.

Out came the by now dog-eared, worn and parted on the folds, map. No roads or any detail other than a different colour for each country like the map you were given to look at in school in the first geography lesson. We needed to sort out the plan for where we should head next. No trains, so we discover. The cheapest method being short of cash was to hitch a lift as we had done previously wherever possible. There were vehicle wrecks strewn along the road, some recent and many others had been there for years. On the road from the airport, we had seen the vehicles and the vivid example of the type of trip we would expect along with the antics of the locals from whom we could hitch a ride and didn't fancy that at all. Violent movements from side to side across the road which seemed to happen for no apparent reason, which could only mean that each time it happened, the driver had lost concentration and jerked the steering wheel to get back on their side of the road. The wrecks were evidence of where many had their thinking stray or nodded off or whatever and not managed to get things back on track. Sometimes, very occasionally you may see that in Europe but the truck behind us from the airport must have done it more than a dozen times as he was talking to his passenger beside him. That coupled with seeing the same a few times from the oncoming traffic, missing us by fractions was almost sure to mean pending disaster which it had been in the past, evidenced by the wrecks. Looking at the faces of the drivers, firstly, we didn't have any confidence in them stopping and secondly they were not the sort you would want to sit next to for any period, if at all. We arrived in the city outside the airline office and decided it was just not worth the risk of that mode of travel.

So how were we to do this, the bus maybe? Still, subject to the perils of the primitive roads and thoughtless driving but at least a bus had a bit of its own weight if in a shunt of some kind. Neither of us had a clue but, as in previous times, we had to make a start somewhere. Chris's sense of direction, which was the subject of scores of arguments by now, was little to none existent. The bit that made it worse was, he thought it was impeccable. He could walk into a shop from one direction and on the way out would swear blind that he had come in from the other side. How we managed to agree on the right way fails me. He was always convincing, but usually, it was me having enough conviction to set off and wait until he followed. After that, it was a myriad of, "Well it could have been from the other way and we just walked around the block. It would have taken less time my way," and so on. Silver-tongued, he had many attributes but a sense of direction wasn't one, it was fatal when combining this with him not giving up even when he was blatantly dead in the water, we would both end up delirious or falling about laughing. Regrouping or recalculating was 80% of our normal day, never boring.

We started to ask people; it was quite a time before we found someone with some English, enough to give directions to the bus terminus. In the process, it was hilarious watching Chris animatedly tried to describe the getting on a bus and sitting down and ringing the bell etc. unashamedly taking the mickey. As with many other times of trying to communicate, we both laughed nervously hoping they didn't think we were laughing at them and take offence. Weaving our way through many more people, every bit as desperate as the rest along the edge of the mud street turning as per the directions for the ten minutes or so it took to get there. We fixed the tickets after a little help from people in the queue but still not convinced, even as the clerk told us that they were the correct tickets, they would take us in the right direction. After all, they didn't have England printed on them which would have made them pretty convincing and, as we had learned to date if they didn't, that could mean we were off to anywhere and anyhow. Still, we would find out in the morning when we would board the bus as there was one scheduled with seats available, lucky as it was one of only two each week. The hotel we found close to the bus station, within a few metres, for the princely sum of ten pence each for the night. We guessed from the price, the accommodation wasn't going to be anything special. We had been in some not so special places before but this was very much more alien and hostile than we expected. The guy from the desk led us to the room.

Having spent time shooting and fishing in an outdoor youth in England, we had experienced all manner of severe weather conditions stuck somewhere in the cold, rain or fog etc., but this insecure, uneasy feeling was like nothing else before, not just the severe elements, there was something more menacing. I had to stop myself thinking about it just as another 'guest' arrived and lay down on one of the other beds in the room accompanied by the same 'manager' who had escorted us to the room. A while earlier at the entrance on the ground floor, he had assured us that we had the room to ourselves as a security measure and so I complained. I have no idea what he said in return in an aggressive, shrill voice, but Chris said to leave it as, regardless and just the same as the other rooms along the corridor, there was no door in the doorway, so how secure was that anyway? We nervously chuckled at the stupidity, much the same as most of the time in recent weeks. The laughter must have been contagious as the new 'guest', who blatantly didn't speak a word of English seemed to pick up on the situation and laughed too. Maybe he was just as nervous, altogether a highly unlikely situation anyway, two Englishmen laughing at themselves in the middle of the night in such a ram shackled area of the city was enough for him to think that the world had gone mad; we certainly did. Maybe the guy was just nuts and laughed at anything. I felt a little more settled but still very wary of the whole night ahead. We both wondered why the other guy wasn't cold with his teeth chattering as ours were.

Outside of the 'hotel', down one flight of broken, UK health and safety field day wooden stairs, it was completely alien and worrying. Other places we had been through were a bit ram-shackled but here had a completely different dangerous aspect to it. We arrived a few days before their New Year; many people had come out of the wilderness and mountains for the celebrations. It was wild. Some of the muddy streets lined with boardwalks buzzing with life. People roughly and heavily dressed for the cold, walked up and down chattering noisily. Every word seemed loaded with aggression and every conversation an argument. Tribesmen rode up and down the streets on horseback at speed in their fur hats and fur coats adorned with pistols, rifles and bullet belts over each shoulder crossing on their chests. It was just like the movies, but it wasn't, this time it was real…and we were right in the middle of it! What part would we play and more importantly just how were our parts to pan out for us? All we knew was that we were going to be the survivors, but until a bit better-detailed plan came together, we would have to wing it as was the usual state of affairs from the first day we set out some weeks ago.

They were all chanting and shouting. I asked Chris if he was scared, he said that maybe that's just the way they acted here in such an extreme and tough environment. He, like me, had a concern in his voice which translated into him speaking unusually sensibly. "I am trying to remember a place that's very similar, I think on Saturday night in Glasgow," he blurts.

"Yes," I say, "but none of them are tooled up as well as the jocks." The two of us tucked up and the second bout of laughter from our new guest in the room reminded us that even there, almost at the top of the world and extreme circumstances, laughter seemed to be a universal language and as contagious here as anywhere else. Thank goodness, generally, we could create some and always hoped that it wouldn't be taken the wrong way given that 99% of the people didn't have any English at all. We agreed that it was us that got ourselves into the situation and that it was only us that would get us out of it. We rested back and tried to relax rather than let our fears define the near future. It wasn't the first time we had been through a similar routine albeit somewhat different this time. By now we didn't even need to say what we were already thinking; 'convince yourself that all is ok'. Although we had been soaking up completely different environments and situations, learning exponentially over the last weeks, both knew this was the furthest we had been outside of our pre-trip, partially naïve daily comfort zone. With a head full of wary thoughts, we tried to sleep, cautious that other guy in the room could have been a murderous maniac and kill us in our sleep merely for the tickets we had bought. He had a bit of a 'Deliverance' look to him.

We must have dropped off for a while until Chris's alarm went off and, surprised and enthusiastic that after dozing, through some good grace we were still in one piece and not robbed; we were off to start the next leg. The other guy in the room never stirred to see us go. On the way out, taking care not to break our necks on the UK safety inspectors' birthday of a staircase. Some steps were almost completely missing. We stared around as if we could still be attacked at any minute thinking ourselves lucky to get so far. Now we were outside and headed to the terminus within sight of the hotel.

Were we really in Kabul and leaving on a bus at 5.30 in the morning for Kandahar on route to Herat? And where the hell is this Herat that was on the ticket anyway? We had to pass through these places on the first leg and second leg of the trip on the way to Iran. Our map didn't have such finite details so, for now, we would have to rely on the organisation of the bus company, bit of a risk but let's see how this pans out.

Chapter 1
Itchy Feet

One summer morning I was 'behind the counter' (as Gran used to call it, kind of officially on serving duty) in my grandmothers' shop. One of the local customers, always up for a laugh, came in and asked if we had any loose peanuts, I say, "No we are all out, but I have some rather promiscuous Brazils if I can interest you." She collapsed into laughter along with four or five customers waiting in the queue, still before 9.30am, bleary-eyed from the previous night in the pub, it was early doors for jocularity, but that event set the tone for the day which was now shaping up to be normally hilarious.

It was interesting how all of the people in the shop knew every word said and generally, all present picked up on what was happening with everyone else. Not at all in any nosey sense, everyone in the shop was included by default just because they were there at the time. Most customers knew each other and were acquaintances if not friends and neighbours and some related. They knew from experience in passing through the shops around all, locals and visitors alike, enjoyed the light-hearted banter that we all encouraged to pass the time. There was a sense of community and everyone, or most everyone picked up on that feeling of confidently being among others with a similar outlook and thinking. Yes, of course, there was the rivalry about who had the biggest house or best car or whatever but all had for a goodly part of the time, an appreciation of the value of harmless fun. They were aware of each other and not so self-indulgent. For me, it was all part of helping people to be at ease so they had a good feeling about coming in and parting with cash for what they wanted. Didn't have to but we would rather have it that way around and them come to us rather than spend somewhere else. Customer relations was an attitude and not a department.

No matter how many people were in the shop, often people queuing outside the door, there was always time and interest and appreciation of a bit of humour. Gran didn't take part as she had no time for such mirth and would complain that we were keeping others waiting not seeing that, apart from the quality of the food which was always the best and impeccable, it was another reason that kept people coming in to spend happily. She had worked hard since leaving school and pretty much thought that was all there was in life, if it wasn't difficult and serious it wasn't right or worth doing. If any good came out of working i.e. having a bit of fun, what you earned wasn't deserved. Real and purposefully old school, grandad, her husband, was knocked out by a falling side of beef in a freezer and accidentally locked in, he was discovered milliseconds before he was completely frozen to death. After that, he had some serious mental issues having had a partially frozen brain or the like and spent the rest of his life in a home. Maybe he did it on purpose to get away from gran who without putting a finer point to, could be a bit of a battle axe. I wouldn't have blamed him if he had. He had a life of Old Riley in the very exclusive home, being tended by nurses. I could see the attraction because as kids we used to visit him.

Left on her own, with three sons and a daughter, she had beaten herself up in the job for 50 years and whoever hadn't gone through the same experience didn't deserve to eat. She certainly was a character and the subject of a few leg-pulls because of her toughness. It was tough on her, me coming along and taking it all light-heartedly and getting attention. She was relentless, never let her guard down and never wasted a thing. If on Saturday evening there was anything left that wouldn't be good for next week, by Sunday night, it was transformed and made into potherbs, jam or lemon curd, meringue or a fruit or fish pie ready to be sold on Monday morning. By lunchtime, every bit was gone. It was almost like a New Year sale opening day, but weekly, with folks scrambling to buy whatever was there. Everyone loved what she made, good wholesome food without wasting a scrap. It wasn't just the ingredients that made it taste good; it was her thought in making use of everything and graft and fervour that gave it all some extra unique flavour. She would rather drink a pint of cyanide than put anything in the bin, that was throwing profit away, and she wasn't having any of it.

My father had packed in his building company due to the recession. After an illness and now really too old to have to put in so many hours, Rose couldn't run the show herself, and it was a good idea for him to take over and she would work part-time. The shop was doing well and he married his second wife, Mari. Mari sold her business in Blackburn, they moved and bought a new house, they both went to work in the shop each day. She, a small woman of Irish descent knew hard work but enjoyed the good life from her efforts. Gran used to think she was a foreigner that had highjacked her favourite son's affections; she had her ideas on how to run a business that didn't hang with Gran. A great formula for trouble and, if anyone was going to win, it was Gran. Mari couldn't help but notice her possessiveness with her son, even at his and her age, as did everyone else, friends, family and customers alike. It constantly niggled Mari to distraction. There was a string of rows between Gran and Mari both with fiery characters and something had to give or, by that stage, go and Gran made sure it was going to be Mari. All she did was to keep on raising the anti and winding her up. On Mari's day off she would go the hairdressers and manicure/pedicure and other pampering shops after generally tidying up and putting the house in order. Dad went home in the evening, opened the door to find there wasn't a stick of furniture left, it was empty. Without any warning or hint at all, instead of filling her day in the usual way, she had packed everything up and gone. I don't know how much if any effort he put into repairing things, he was so beside himself with her leaving. Knowing him, not much, I would expect; he knew the problem with Gran and the upshot was that, was the end. They sorted out the financials through lawyers and I don't think they saw each other again.

I had been working in London for a builder's merchant (after one or two other jobs) when he called me back to help him. It took some deliberation, things were going quite nicely and I was well thought of by those at the traditional family company I was working for. I sat and talked with the director who was the eldest family member in the company and after explaining the offer from my father he gave me the blessing to leave. After all, in a somewhat larger business, he had been in the same situation with his father many years ago. So eventually I agreed and came back to, what was in my mental justification, a little light entertainment with the regular customers some of whom I had known since I was a child. I didn't see it as a strong career move, at that stage of life there was plenty of time to see how the situation fitted with me and see how it developed at the same time as helping my father. So long as he and I spent plenty of time apart outside of work, I could see it working in some fashion.

For a time it was fun. As Gran had been there for many years, she knew everyone and their families and they, in turn, knew all of us. They and their by now not so young daughters, some of whom were well worth attention, were a constant source of amusement and things to do socially along with reconnecting with other school chums. Not a day went by without some leg pulling along the way from other shopkeepers and customers alike; it was standard practice to regularly tease them back and have them believe all sorts of nonsense.

There was also, of course, the daily lunchtime spectacle of the girls from Elmsleigh School. 6th formers in their white blouses, by now after a few minutes' walk from the school, their ties around their waists. An extra button open at the blouse neck and gymslips now rolled up around the waist to make them shorter (rolled down again and ties back on before going back through the school gates). They would swarm the wide pavements on Whitegate Drive looking for attention. They got it, and why not? It was a treat each day that I tried not to miss, avoiding any deliveries away from the shop to be around that time. As interesting if not a little more so, occasionally I would catch a glimpse of a girl from an office across the road, she was quite something to behold. At the front of the shop there was always a display of bedding plants or whatever was in season taking up an area of the broad pavement. I would go out there to make sure that all was in order, it was a good excuse to take some air and see who was out and about. She was Norma, a comptometer operator in an accountancy firm office over a shop across the road. We saw each other several times in passing from a distance just smiling and saying hi. I kind of assumed, as I had seen a youngish guy drop her off a couple of times, that she was in a relationship.

The first time we met to speak was in the bakers maybe 50 metres from the shop. There was quite a queue, she smiled over my way as I was about to be served. Silvia, the lady behind the counter sort of winked at me and signalled over to Norma as if to say that she and I ought to get together and asked what I would like. Feeling a bit frisky after the earlier approving look from Norma I said, "Give me three loaves and five fish, and fifty thousand people out of the audience please Silvia."

Silvia chuckled and wryly quipped, "Look, I can do the bread but you're going to have to go back to your shop for the fish and maybe Bloomfield Road (the football ground) for the rest," knowingly and knowing that I was showing off a bit for Norma's benefit. Norma spluttered too and the other customers laughed. She, by now, was served by one of the other girls as I paid for the bread (three loaves as it happened, that's what made me think of the quip) and I walked with her back to her office. As we left the bakers it was obvious that all of them, staff and customers alike were talking about us. It was as if they had all conspired for us to meet and get together, of course they had, that was what they were like. In time, it was quaint how they enjoyed and showed they supported us together. It turned out that she and the guy I had seen drop her at work were not together, he was the son of a close family friend who spent time with Norma's family and not her type to the dismay of the mother. He didn't figure at all from that day.

Life was picking up and looking good. Maybe it was a good idea after all to leave the life I had made in the East End of London and clandestinely there was something better on the horizon.

A girl with a sharp wit, pretty good looking and a comely girl with a broad, genuine disarming smile that uncovered bright and characterful, slightly overlapping, uneven white teeth. A little shorter than me, she had an hourglass figure and masses of dark curly hair to below her shoulders and a fringe that somehow pointed you directly to her deep brown eyes. Always looked impeccable, well dressed in co-ordinated clothes often hot pants or a short skirt and boots, not too much or overly done but carefully constructed make-up, she was lovely and available, I was willingly hooked. We clicked straightway from the day in the bakers, dated and ended up being a couple much to the delight of all the local customers and business people alike. We enjoyed similar things, except the barleywine that is which she loved and was the cornerstone of several of rows and late night flying objects, ashtrays etc., it gave her the opportunity to show the fiery side of her character. Love a girl with spirit! It looked like we would stay together, so it seemed.

Gran's traditional fresh fish, fruit and vegetable shop had been there for ions with her in it. In the South Shore area of Blackpool near Stanley Park, it worked well, busy and reasonably profitable through long working hours. Mostly bigger than average Accrington brick built buildings in the area, the shop was towards the end of a row of about twenty others. At the other end was the tram sheds built many years ago in the early nineteen hundreds and owned by the town corporation. Across the road, with the two-way tram tracks in the centre which guided the trams to Blackpool centre, was another similar parade of shops of the various kinds you would find serving a local community. An affluent area, the surrounding houses were quality built and occupied by doctors, lawyers, business people, entertainers and celebrities. Very busy in the summer months also with people from the famed Blackpool shows on the Piers, the Winter Gardens and the Blackpool Tower buildings. One of Blackpool's claims to fame was that The Tower design was by Alexandre Gustave Eiffel, which not many people know or believe but it's true, with similar features to the more famous Eiffel Tower of Paris. Unlike Paris, the general attitude of the tourists in Blackpool was more akin to candy floss and 'kiss me quick' hats and family beach days than fine Parisian qualities, but that doesn't mean that they didn't know how to have fun. To bring the people from inland into the town there were three train stations. Each with many excursion platforms to carry thousands of families each year from the inland cotton and wool towns on their annual two week holidays.

Having a zany bunch of entertainer characters around the shop accentuated a bizarre atmosphere the area took on. Comedians, of which there were many, not all professionals in the shows, clowns and magicians, high wire performers, dancers and singers, lion tamers from the zoo and all types of professional people along with a few footballers too. Blackpool's football ground, Bloomfield Road was only about one mile away. Scores of characters in the area with 'out of the ordinary' lifestyles gave birth to tales and idiosyncrasies that were a continual source of interesting conversation and amusement among the good-humoured customers and other shopkeepers. Stories about and from famous people who returned to do the summer seasons year after year spread from one shop to another quicker than truths but all for the best possible motives and in the name of fun and a spirit of the local community. No doubt some of these interactions with locals became material to be included in their shows.

Alice with her white stick had lived there for years was now in the old folks' home. She used to sing and dance in the shows. From all accounts she was good looking and a bit of a lass in her time. Although now as blind as a bat (hence the stick), but for some reason, miraculously she could still spot me from scores of yards away, would straighten herself up as if she was 18 years old from the aged usually bent posture of 85 or so and blurt in a shrill voice. "Sonny Jim, sonny Jim," she'd shriek, that was what she always called me, everyone within earshot knew what was coming next, "Can you see me across the road?"

My stock response as always was, "Yes, of course, I can see you Alice, plain as day." Every time she asked I'd say the same and every time she'd laugh and say, "You know what I mean you cheeky monkey." You could never get one word of sense from her apart from that request for help and surely when she would buy some fruit, she'd record the price and count every penny in change. She was a wry, seemingly batty old girl and one of the priceless characters in a community of residents and shopkeepers and had a spirit which this typified. Other people around knew the routine and laughed along with it. Even Jack Day, the miserable butcher (I've never met a jolly one), just by his shop was where Alice would scream from having just turned the corner out of the Home, would chuckle at the exchange being cautious not lop off his finger hacking up pork chops. "For crying out loud, will you come and help her before she's run over," he would say chuckling at the repetitiveness of the once or twice daily event as if it had never happened before.

Ted Tatlock, an old boy, must have been 80 if he was a day. He had a small holding, every day he would come in his rusty old Austin A30 van that I am sure was never insured or maintained, with small amounts of different vegetables for sale. He had a weather-worn face, a bit rusty like his van, and deep wrinkles around his eyes and brow. He was from Marton Moss, an area known for small-time growers and a place occupied by several let's say unique individuals that spent most of their time there…and only there. Ted had known Gran and the family for 50 years. He had little else to pay other than the electricity bill with money and Gran in her shop and a few others along the way were a source of small cash. Someone had tapped into the water main supply many years ago, everyone needs it and it comes from the sky for free, so they worked out a way of it being for free to several plots along the lane. They were not gipsies, just local growers having survived throughout the war and made cash from selling goods outside of rationing. Virtually all the buildings (of sorts) were illegal; some had caravans, tax were the things holding down the felt on the roof. It was a sort of situation where they didn't bother anyone, so nobody bothered them. They all had a good and convincing argument for why and how they did things and people wishing to go in there to reorganise things from say, the local council or any authority, didn't want to hear it for the sake of their sanity and not wanting to waste days. All the food Ted needed, he grew and if there were something else he wanted, he would horse trade with other neighbouring smallholders that did have it.

My aunt also had quite a large nursery there with many greenhouses growing flowers, chrysanthemums, sweet peas and stocks for part of the year and salad items of tomatoes and lettuce etc., at other times. For Hazel, it was a proper business and unlike most of the other smaller plots, it wasn't just sustenance. As such she and her husband Harry were revered by others and indeed she was a fine woman. Harry was a Freemason and Hazel was one of the first women Freemasons certainly in the area. When she died at a ripe old age after a wholesome and healthy life, the female masonic lodge supplied a 20 strong 'guard of honour' to see her off. A token of how well they thought of her. As a family, we were all fairly well known in the surrounding area, each one taking time regularly to remind the others of each of the other's reputations.

It was a depressing time economically and to top it all, we had power cuts. Arthur Scargill and a bunch of other union cronies were determined to break the country creating all types of endurance tests for the British public to suffer. No wonder we as late teens needed some excitement in our lives. No wonder we relished fast cars and even faster women, nightclubs, music and dancing and such. Who wouldn't want such distractions with this doom and gloom backdrop to our lives?

-oo-

There was a squeal of tyres, the shop door opened and a hand appeared holding one of those new-fangled car keys, they looked new-fangled and to be from a Jaguar. Friend for years, Chris was the next bit to appear through the door with a big grin on his face. He worked in the local car distributors and he had just been on a demonstration with a prospective buyer for a new V12 E-type Jaguar. It was that mid-blue colour; the ultimate top of the range prestige driving machine of the time, every lad and dad wanted one. A machine to behold and determined to make the most of it, he was beholding it so much on the way back to the dealership, he stopped off to let me behold it too and have a demonstration. After all, he had a duty to show it to anyone who wanted to buy it and I sure as hell 'wanted' to buy it just as much as anyone else. Whether I had the where with all to do so was nothing to do with it at all.

After flooring the throttle from the side street, the back of the car skidded out across the white centre line and the steel tram tracks buried in the main road. Whitegate Drive was a very wide road which accommodated the tram tracks. Duly opposite locking to regain control, both of us with broad grins on our faces thinking we were great, it skidded back across to the opposite side sliding sideways down the street. After repeating this several times before we gained back full traction approaching 60 mph, both with broad grins on our faces, turned onto the main Preston road where three or four times we approached the speed of sound and almost took off before the adrenalin rush forced me to ease off the throttle.

We were youths out for a bit of ill thought out fun? Never in a month of Sundays would we do such a thing! Gambling with death and displaying irresponsible and abandoned excitement? Not in the least! What else could you call it but fun? That we were a danger to ourselves and the whole surrounding community and running the risk of destroying a new top of the range, telephone number priced car, never even came into our thinking. Anyway, no doubt Norma working in the accountants' office on the first floor across the road would have seen us in the first part of our jaunt. She missed very little activity in the vicinity, being a little possessive, was particularly vigilant at lunchtime, she saw the dangers attached to when the school girls were around; by that time we were a regular number. It must have been very difficult if not impossible to miss this spectacle of the screaming, bright blue V-12 E-type with its screeching tyres disappearing in a cloud of blue tyre smoke and zigzag lines of black rubber etched on to the road. It was another normal day on the Drive.

The same happened time after time with new 'flying machines' throughout the summer; test drives always took a little longer than normal as there was always someone else he could show the car to that 'wanted to buy'. Out of the blue one day, abruptly and mercilessly, Chris was fired. None of us could appreciate why they dismissed him at the time, after all, we were only having a bit of fun. That it was outrageously dangerous, unforgivable and very expensive if things went wrong, never crossed our minds. Just kids finding a way past the national depression that certainly was not down to our doing. Admittedly, he could have been a little more diligent when he opened the door to get out of another new car and a car came along and took it straight off. No one could see how on earth he could be blamed for such a thing, after all, the other car was speeding, and no one was hurt! It was completely understandable and not irresponsible as the chief honcho at the distributors called it. He had no sense of adventure, or humour. It could have happened to anyone. Mind you, it didn't go down well constantly picking the flashiest car in the showroom as a weekend smoker. One time he took a client's Aston and was seen with it by the owner out drinking at a country pub. The jury was still out on this one when he dove at speed into a flood in which it sunk up to the windows and as good as wrote off another new car. It was unfathomably the last straw. Completely bewildering that they treated him that way.

Some months before this we started to think about doing something completely different. At first, it was as a joke, you know over a game of snooker. "Hellfire, things are so depressing (the light over the snooker table along with those in the rest of the pub went out due to a power cut from the miners' strike) we might as well emigrate!"

"Even if we have to put up with a few impudent colonials, it's better than putting up with a communist union leader bringing the country to its knees."

"Well, one thing is for sure," says 'Young' Harold my partner in the snooker in the four-hand game, "if you decide to go anywhere with Chris, you'll be lucky to get beyond the end of the Highcross Road here with his sense of direction."

I say, "Yeah well I'm relying on my own to get us through and just keep his contribution in the back of my mind," as I snookered him badly and we both laughed. How right he would be in the long run and how many times did his words flood back into mind. Both him and his father, 'Big' Harold had an endearing knack for stating the obvious, loaded with wit which somehow managed to resonate from time to time throughout the rest of your life.

Suddenly emigrating wasn't such a daft idea. We were young and carefree; it was the very idea of a trip that reminded us of the fact; why not experience what it's like in another country far away. Canada was the first choice but having applied for there, Australia and South Africa, Australia came back and said we were accepted. Imagine all sorts of discord and stressful conditions around us politically and economically and suddenly we have the opportunity to go halfway around the world for ten quid! We'll have some of that, thank you very much! "Little competition for ideas for doing anything else," says Chris.

"I can't think of one," I said. Decision made.

"Taking into consideration Chris's employment record to date, emigrating wasn't such a bad idea," a friend chipped in. Trust them to say it succinctly. By that stage, we were only leaving the country because Chris couldn't get a job in the whole of England and for sure absolutely nothing to do with cars. After convincing my father it was part of the growing up process (he never forgave me for passing up the then family business) we accepted and waited for a date to leave opting for going by boat to take a cruise for few weeks as the start of our new adventure.

Then came the time to let Norma in on the plan, ugh! To soften the blow, we had been thinking about it before we met (we had to a degree albeit flippantly until the off, where it became real) and it all just came together now at our stage of involvement as a rather tough coincidence for both of us. Eventually, after discussions, the plan was for her to come out when I had settled. It never came to that as the story will tell and on reflection, I don't think she ever really forgave me for leaving her even though we spoke by phone and wrote often.

I had many second thoughts over both my father and Norma, particularly over Norma. I had become very used to her and she was a lot to leave behind. We were given a date to leave in some six weeks' time and made plans on that basis. Chris and I both knew each other's families and discussed the subject of 'should or shouldn't we' with them and friends but it always came out the same. If we didn't do it now, probably we would never. We would spend the rest of the time wondering what it would have been like and what an opportunity we would have missed. If either of us had dropped out, the other wouldn't have gone. It's something you do with your mate or mates or spouse, not alone. In the main, it was probably this fact that kept us in the idea that we were making the right decision and eventually made us up sticks and go. On top of this, Chris also had a girlfriend, who was quite tasty, that he also thought something of. When he told her about the trip, she said, if he were to go, she would rather finish the relationship than wait for him to travel around and then until he came back. After that, I could hardly have bailed out then after an upheaval of that degree on his part.

On a Tuesday evening, we had a phone call from the guy at the Australian embassy. We had the booking on the boat but they had a cancellation for that Friday, two seats on a plane were available and we could take these instead of sailing. It was a bit of a shock, the realisation that for sure now it was happening. It wasn't just a lad's fairy tale where all our mates from the pub would take the mickey saying we were dreamers. Most didn't think we would do it when it came finally making the decision. After some deliberation, we agreed to take the flight and packed for leaving. In the long run, it was a good idea as it made time available for our goodbyes much shorter which eased the pain, especially with Norma. The adventure was about to start. Over those few days, we still had to shore each other up as the deliberation was still going on in our minds as we played out daily life. Friends would ask if we were still going and each time they did we would sink into the same thoughtful state.

Chapter 2
Boogie Street

We had no idea what it would be like there in Australia having missed all the briefs and chats we should have had in the normal scheme of things. We had accepted their offer of leaving on short notice and now there was no time for lectures and orientation meetings, etc. We didn't even research Australia before we applied. Hellfire, what for, we were going to give it a whirl whatever. It didn't seem worth it until we were accepted for us to build up hopes and plans if it wasn't going to happen. Leading up to the time it all came together there were severe financial and public disturbances etc., in the UK with the miners' strike and its knock-on effects. Some things were tough but I was still working with plenty of social things for amusement.

The thoughts of the trip were bobbing along in the back of our minds until the ship departure date until changing to flying; suddenly it was time to leave. We asked many questions of the guy from the immigration but didn't have a lot of response during those few days before leaving. We started thinking that through the haste to fill the seats; we had just been making up the numbers so to speak. Maybe the embassy staff had quotas for getting people there and hurriedly they had slotted us in without thinking things through. Maybe they were commissioned on the number of people they managed to send there? Well, whatever, we were up for it and nothing was going to change that now. We didn't have enough time to contemplate an alternative, maybe that was a bonus for them knowing that, as in the case of the cancellation that made the fights available to us at the last minute, some people do change their minds.

Someone would meet us at the airport (we had opted to go to Perth in Western Australia for some reason that fails me now, maybe it was because it was a young city that may have presented more opportunities work-wise) and that this person would arrange everything. They would organise hotel until we found jobs and a place to live. And that was that. We didn't think such an arrangement was excessively good of them. It was them taking us halfway around the world to a strange country because they needed people. A country never progresses and prospers with a static or shrinking population. It was their idea for us to go through need. So they should make sure we were ok and settled. We found out much later that they rushed us through as the whole assisted passage system was to be abandoned because there were financial and employment problems looming there. We were told later after arrival by the agent we met that we were some of the very last people to be taken on that scheme. Not such a good start for our prospects but we thought we could cope with a bit of luck.

In what seemed to be moments we were on the train spending a very quiet first couple of hours on route to London. It was real now and finally sinking in that very soon we would be doing things and living a life that would be completely different than what we were used to doing. No more having a beer and a game of snooker with friends that we had known for as long as we could remember. No more games of darts and joking about how bad we were at it. The jokes when we missed a sitter of "Your tea is ready" were changed suddenly for "Thank god we don't have to put up with that for much longer, soon the Australians will have to". It was altogether now with a bit of a different tone but still with an endearing humour. We had grown up in this community experiencing all the things that kids do along with other events, some contrived and some by accident, which was all unique to us. It was all we knew but it was what kept us and our peers amused. Their attitude change and reference to our upcoming trip was a way of slotting into their thinking that we were going and in a way accepting and taking part in it. What would our friends think about us when we were gone, what would they say to each other about us picking up and clearing off? You could think that we had left in part because we were bored with them. What would they be like when we arrived back, how would they have changed, how would we have changed and how would we then view what we had left behind on our return from travelling.

We decided that whatever was going to happen we would deal with it and be happy with our choice no matter what they thought. It can't be such a bad thing to have the experience, 'broadening our horizons', as they all said and exercising our minds in such a way. We still felt a little uneasy as to how we would think of the people who had not done what we were now doing to the extent that we were bothered if we would still be friends as a result of going. Just having gone through the experience of applying and deciding to go, brought about a different way of thinking that made us in a way different. Not bigger or better or smarter, just different. Strange the things you think about. It took a while to convince ourselves not to be concerned about it and say that what would be would be because we were going, for sure, no going back, it was happening. We were actually on our way.

We arrived at Euston station. I had lived in London for a while and was used to the tube etc. and managed to find the right train to Heathrow. Chris had never flown before. I had spent several years in the Air Training Corps and had flown many times training in small aircraft. However, I had never been on a commercial airliner or even into an airport to see what happens there. I guess through nerves and bravado we joked with the airline staff and told them we hadn't flown before and they should take particular care with us. Extra food and drinks and much more attention from the stewardesses would be appreciated, and not wasted on two good-looking young guys. We never thought for a minute that they had heard it all before, as it was a first time for us clearly it was a new experience for them and certainly a privilege for them to have us there.

Down the corridors and along walkways in the airport and suddenly we were inside the plane. It was a Boeing 707, whatever that meant. Our seats were close to the back as of course back then smoking was allowed, within a short time, we were trundling down the runway at what we thought breakneck speed. It was almost as fast as that day in the V12 E-type on Preston New Road. It was exciting, a whole new world, a new way of getting somewhere…and we still had no clue as to what it would be like when we did get there. It was all part of the fun and the nervousness and anticipation of the unknown heightened the mood.

We landed in Rome, both still struggling with the pressure in our ears, to allow passengers off and in what seemed to be one or two hours we are ready for the off. The captain chirps up to tell us that there was a technical problem and there would be a delay in taking off. Well, that was a bit of a blow, wound up like two coiled springs after the first take-off and landing and still with ear problems. "A technical problem?" says Chris in horror. When he was nervous or excited he would chew the inside of his cheek. "It worked 100% on the way here," he gasped. Thinking about the odds, the last time we did take off it worked, now the odds have now shortened somewhat, only one success out of two attempts. We glance at each other, both with the same question in mind, how the hell did that happen? Car engines can have problems with which we had experience but this sophisticated piece of kit must have had scores more components. Up until then, we didn't have the slightest notion that planes had technical faults much less it happens to the one *we* were on! Through rank fear, in nervous jest, we talked to the girls asking them to make doubly sure that whatever the problem was, we were rooting for them. Please would they see it is properly repaired before we went through that noisy rumbling, engine screeching stuff again because this time, in light of the problem, these things have technical problems 50% of the time. We took off once and it was ok, we try it again and there is a problem? The next thing we know maybe the possibility of a technical problem at three million feet or whatever was the acceptable flying height (or whatever it's called). At the time, of course, it took hundreds of words, most of them incoherent and jumbled causing some laughter among other passengers. By now the stewardesses had realised they had a bit of a handful with two aviation novices, desperately fighting back the laughter and trying to be polite without losing it. They knew we weren't offensive or obnoxious, just using humour to overcome our serious apprehensiveness and nerves. Both they and passengers were within a hairsbreadth of wetting themselves in shrieks of laughter at the back of the plane at our reality of breakdowns occurring half of the time.

Things calmed a little while I explained some thoughts from my Air Training Corps days about how planes fly with lift from the wings etc. He kept on, "Technical problem?" By that time, even though we had flown to get to where we were, the whole idea of flight came back into question. This thing was so big, all that weight, the people and the baggage? Is it possible, safely! In cars, of which we had many that had 'technical problems' breaking down on motorways and such, at least you were not three million or whatever feet up in the air. Even from ten feet up there would be a bit of a mess if it fell, let alone from tens of thousands more feet in the sky brought more shrieks of laughter from the passengers and stewardesses.

It helped only a little, one of the girls managed to hold herself long enough to speak without bursting into laughter saying that generally most problems, an involuntary guffaw, with planes happen while they are on the ground. "Phew," says Chris with a wry smile, "put another scotch in my glass to take the edge off my hyperactive thoughts while I count that one small mercy."

We had been on the tarmac for hours but a few stressful moments later we were off down the runway in complete darkness which was another new, fleetingly quipped upon, experience and we were in the air without incident. Phew! We slept for a while. By now we were several hours late on our way to Singapore. There was some talk of stopping in India but we carried on straight through. The deliberation was the pilot trying to make his mind up if we needed to refuel, "Let's hope he gets that one right," says Chris nervously as we chatted to the stewardess. Because of the hullabaloo from earlier, the male stewards joined in not wanting to miss out on the opportunity to flex their cerebral prowess. They were pretty much openly gay and liked the banter. I could see it all brewing with Chris and his razor wit as Jeremy cuts in, "You two boys look like you are out for some fun."

"Well, it has been known Jeremy," as he spots his name on the lapel badge.

"Of course when we get to Singapore we will be late so in all probability, you will have missed your connection and have to stay at least one night. I have some great places for you to try," as Jeremy with the skill of a ballet dancer deftly hands a gin and tonic to the guy across the aisle, winking at him and showing how pleased he was to serve him. Both of us amused at his gestures, looked at each other wondering what's going to come next having now confirmed his persuasion. "You should try Boogie Street as it's your first time there," winking at the leggy blond stewardess that had a warm but yearning to be official smile each time she walked by. From the gesture she made to him not to encourage us we suspected he was in the process of setting us up for something. Minutes later he passes again, "There are some wild spots but there are worst places to go. If you do decide to it would be best if you didn't wear your best clothes and shoes," he pauses again, "oh and leave your watch in the hotel rather than lose it."

Chris chirps, "Um, all sounds a bit rough and racy for a delicate thing such as yourself Jeremy." The blond guffaws almost choking for breath and the redhead covers her mouth both trying to control themselves and the food trays they are handing out, both fearful of even glancing over in case they lose it. "Perhaps in your flight bag you have a couple of pairs of gold slingbacks you could lend us." That did it for the blond, she had to go to the galley to wipe the tears from her eyes and compose herself. They all knew this kind of exchange was on its way from the start of the journey. All of us were complete strangers and we would be in each other's company for many hours, better to set the tone as one of humour than anything else. By this time they knew we were capable and cheeky enough to voice all things that people were thinking and be relaxed as this mid-flight scenario continued.

Nervously, not wanting to drop out of the exchange knowing that we were at the very least a challenge he was not sure of winning with, at the same time knowing that we were the customers, Jeremy pirouettes with his tray of whatever, "Well it's certainly different and you'll meet some interesting people, you and your friend might like something out of the ordinary."

"How out of the ordinary," says Chris. "I like the youngish ones, girls over 16 but only just," he adds.

"Well," says Jeremy, "that's not very out of the ordinary, I was thinking of something a bit more diverse."

"Diverse?" I say, "Stops with me at just a hint of fine facial hair and a body like Brigitte Bardot, maybe that's too pedestrian for such a high flyer as you Jeremy?" The blond takes another deep breath trying desperately not to listen for fear that she falls apart as this time Jeremy goes off to the galley hardly containing himself. Chris starts again, "Will the people we meet still have the hospital tags on their wrists from the sex change op?" unwittingly hitting the nail right on the head as we later find out.

"I don't know," he quips, "I don't look at their wrists."

"It won't be their breasts either," cracks Chris as both stewardesses brace themselves trembling in anticipation of what's coming in the next part of his sentence, "unless it's just to remind you of when you were a baby with your mum Jeremy." Chris tries to close Jeremy off and winks at the blond as she looks at me and puts her hand over her mouth again. I could see Chris had already made the plan to strangle Jeremy with the tea towel he had tucked in his belt if he brushed his leg again in passing. It was time to give it a rest; we were all aching from laughing and the strain of trying not to.

We were also exhausted with the mental gymnastics as more continued until the girls had finished with the food and cleared up. I can remember thinking that gays are consummate banterers, almost like born-again Christians, so we find out, it seems impossible for them to resist imparting their idea of how great life is like where they are and they mask this effort with tongue in cheek innuendos where the response is food for their egos. It's funny that they enjoyed the sporting fast chat with those who are not. Harmless as it seems, if you are heterosexual you have a deep fundamental desire for them not to win as heterosexual needs to remain heterosexual. It's funny also that they don't enter into the same banter with women, certainly not so much when there are men around. It was all harmless fun, it did pass some time and created more than a chuckle for those listening; it didn't take too long for the passengers around to twig what was happening. Somehow we had all bonded, not so much with the stewards I hasten to add, we were still a challenge, more so with the girls and the surrounding passengers. Much to the stewardesses' relief, we settled down with another drink the girls were happy to bring for us and slept again. Disappointingly the steward and not the stewardess woke us as we approached Singapore. Probably a wise idea from their point of view, maybe because they were unsure of just how pushy we could be. Maybe it was just policy. To us it was new but to them, all part of a well practised procedure I guessed. A glass of water and a wet face towel to freshen up and before long we were preparing to land, anticipation was running high wondering what was next. It was the first time we stepped off the plane and as we were now in Asia, this was going to be very different. You could feel the huge heat through the sides of the covered gangway, very different. Having flown many times since through varying climates, you take it in your stride but this was the first time of sensing that vastly differing climate change.

Like being in a sauna when you take your first breath after throwing water on the coals the hot and humid air of Singapore involuntarily stunted your breath as we stepped out of the airport building, down the steps from the doors and walked towards the waiting airline bus to take us to the hotel. The procedure had been explained to us on the plane by the attentive stewardesses. They went over it knowing that we had never been in such circumstances before. They took the opportunity to chat and bring some drinks in appreciation of having kept them entertained for a goodly part of the trip.

Everything you touched, the handrails on the steps, the walls and columns were warm. With every step, instantly you could feel the heat from the marble and then the tarmac through the soles of your shoes. The heavy air deadened sounds. In fact, it was so heavy it stopped you thinking about anything else other than the weight of the evening atmosphere, almost to the point where we thought we might have to go back inside to breathe properly again. Within seconds you were wet through, the whole of your shirt and down past the waistband to your trouser pockets were soaking with sweat as we waited for the driver to open the bus.

Wow, there was no real sense of having gone anywhere as all we did was to sit on the plane and now we were somewhere completely different and alien. Yes, we knew we had travelled thousands of miles but there was no real sense of having done so. And yet, here we were in a place far from our imagination with an atmosphere that we were desperately trying to comprehend. Additionally, in setting out from England to go to Australia, we had no idea that we would be visiting anywhere else. Suddenly we found ourselves in Singapore. Everything felt different, the temperature, the humidity and surroundings confirmed you were not home, nowhere near. Like walking out of the Dr Who Tardis onto another planet, it was exciting, fascinatingly different, totally unanticipated and magically happening in front of us. We were both mesmerised with so much to look at so different than what we were used to. Thank goodness we had something organised by the airline because we were in such awe we wouldn't have had a clue what to do.

It was late evening by the time we arrived at the hotel and checked in. The airline had done us proud and especially, all for ten quid. Flown thousands of miles, been fed and given drinks, now booked into an upmarket hotel, meal included. Rather different than ending up on the banks of the Solway with less than 50 pence and sleeping in the pub lounge (it was actually the landlady's lounge as the bar was her house with the beer barrels in the kitchen) and given some stew to tide us over. It had a huge brightly lit reception with a long desk occupied by two uniformed clerks. There was a lift to one side and a staircase to the other. Behind us, where we had walked in was all glass forming the front of the building which was relatively old. I'd say only 20 or so years old and still quite impressive. Mind you, it was a hotel used by the airlines I guess for staff and exactly these times when passengers were unavoidably delayed, missing their connecting flights etc. It had to be pretty near the mark to compensate for whatever problem had befallen their flights. They handed us the keys and a boy led us to the room on the third floor. All quality décor and furniture, well done and expensive but now unashamedly showing its age.

A couple of beers from room service and a shower and we were 'up n at um' ready to have a complimentary meal and then take a taxi to Boogie Street. After we finished dinner which was to die for, we decided to make the most of it and had some oriental type fish with sauce starter and then a steak followed up with strawberries and ice cream all washed down with a bottle of wine. "Well," says Chris, "just the meal was worth all of the ten quid we paid for the trip in one sitting," both sitting back and chuckling. We were getting used to this kind of treatment. The concierge looked sideways at us when we told him the address to give to the cab driver. We should have had more suspicion after the concierge reaction and when the driver asked if we really wanted to go there. He seemed quite switch on and, as he said, he had far better places to take us to go particularly if we wanted women. The clue was in what he just said but once again, we missed it. We were having none of that nonsense, we were sucked right into Jeremy's' plan. Going was part of his dare, so that's where we were off. After all, after the delay, maybe he suffered the same fate and we would see him on the on-going flight. If we did, how could we say we hadn't been? He would never have stopped, telling us how much we missed and we would have had no defence. Little did we know that the next flight was with another airline, we had no way of knowing. Not backing down was a major part of our reason for going there whether we met Jeremy again or not. It's funny what drives you into doing certain things, we never really thought of going anywhere else. The taxi driver was our only other source of information; he knew what we were in for. He also knew that we had no clue as to the nature of what we were going to and had already formulated his plan B. He was used to foreigners and knew they meant money. About forty years old and bigger in stature than most Chinese he was a well-seasoned taxi driver with a paunch. A cigarette in the corner of his mouth was there all the time as he was talking to us, when it burned down it he replaced it. His lips were stained with nicotine as was his moustache. Yes, he was interested in us having a good time but appeared sleazy and more interested in him making money. We made him stick to Jeremy's plan as much through mistrust of him as much as the dare.

We drove down the street where there were colourful, brassy women everywhere. Stark lamps hung illuminating little kiosks and rickety shops selling all manner of weird foods like bugs in sweet jars and manky food hanging as if it had been there for weeks. It probably had. The lights threw shadows of the hanging items that got in its way. There was a packed pathway and then single storey buildings of shops and more food places equally as ram shackled as the barrow/kiosks lining each side of the road. The people milling around and crossing in front of us made it almost impassable as the taxi moved slowly inching its way forward. There were cooking smells wafting in through the part open windows of the taxi mixed with incense and perfume (I think from the tarts) and a hubbub of activity, people weaving themselves through the trails of people coming from the opposite direction on the pathway. There was a continual noise of shrill voices from people arguing or selling their wares and music coming from several places at the same time, each predominant tune getting louder and fading as we passed bars and cafes. Side streets appeared to be the same with many people but just smaller and no doubt murkier.

We drove for some time down the street slowly taking in the sights. What seemed like scores of women tried to hold on to the cab and entice us out but the cab driver kept going saying that, he would drive us the length of the street and after seeing it all, he would leave us at the end. From there we could make up our minds as to whether it was where we wanted to be or somewhere else would be more suitable. We stepped out of the cab and were mobbed by highly painted and what appeared to be brassy but good looking women. They were a sight, exquisitely dressed in brightly coloured skimpy blouses with plunging necklines, which shot down through very little shape (we ignored this at the time) and ultra-short skirts, some with splits to the waist exposing thighs and equally colourful skimpy knickers. The make-up was perfection, heavily painted eyes, lashes and brows, high cheekbones accentuated by face powder or whatever they do and layers of deep red or pink lipstick.

They were good, obviously extremely good at making themselves attractive, past mistresses at creating and accentuating the features maybe they craved to show. Perhaps that's why you want them to be real because they make it that way and want it to be real. The cab driver said that not everything is the way it seemed and asked us to notice the bulges at their crotches. At that point being mauled by several asking, "You want good time Jonny?" still not wanting to believe it was untoward and weird. Fortunately, we got the message jumped back into the cab and fled post haste.

Chris says, "Some of them must be women, they looked so good, quite fancied the one that collared me, they can't all be blokes!" I thought I'd jot that one down for a laugh over a beer with friends or when I come to write my memoirs but I must admit they decked themselves up so well it was almost impossible to tell the difference. The driver explained that they were all men and Boogie Street was well known only for 'ladyboys'. That was enough of that for us two. "Where next?" says Chris after we had hurriedly climbed back into the cab, down to the junction and off the wild street. We both laughed at Jeremy and the sporty exchanges we had on the plane came back into mind and how hilarious it must have been for the stewardesses and him, especially now we realised what he was talking about and what he was setting us up for.

The driver rubbed his hands with glee at the prospect of taking us to his favourite brothel and the chance of him making his commission. We said we wanted to go to a bar first thinking that there may be some females that were not out for business. We came to a stop outside a not very brightly lit bar on a side street, as we walked in a couple of people recognised the driver. It didn't look like we would find what we were looking for in this establishment. As tourists with a taxi driver in a bar not knowing or being involved with anyone else we stood out like sore thumbs as a mark for the driver. There was a couple at one table and three or four men dotted around the place and didn't look like the sort of place that would shape up to be a raucous hotbed of social interaction and fun. We got the impression that it was probably where taxi drivers went for a break or wind down. It was his choice and more than likely a choice with the least chance of other women turning up as that would reduce the chance of a cut from the brothel he was to take us to. After a couple of beers, he took us off to the Asian hen house which he assured was the best in town where the women were beautiful and not too expensive.

We drove again for some time and went into gates of an entrance road leading to a big detached house. There were no lights outside except the red one over the door. The house was wooden with balconies all of which was in dire need of repair, badly fitted rackety shutters with broken louvres. We were talking together on the way in through the door that opened as we approached, it was in very secluded grounds, both of us felt uneasy so much so even on the way in, already we had the notion that we didn't want to stay. There was a huge open area with seats and chairs placed around where some of the girls had been sat chatting to each other. The owner picked out two and they joined a sampling of five or six girls that came from other rooms in front of us. Loaded with bravado on the plane and filled with anticipation in the hotel, it is difficult to explain how a little anxiety can change your whole outlook. With our mood swing, the idea of fun gave way to a feeling of being taken on. Rather than us being there to enjoy ourselves, we were overwhelmed with their purpose of collecting money. Suddenly after the initial eye contact from the parade of wanton women, none of them appealed. Perhaps because of this feeling of being pressed which led to unease, it began to feel intimidating so we decided to leave completely turned off. The owner protested and unbuttoned his jacket revealing a pistol saying that we must stay and enjoy ourselves having come so far and the taxi driver having made such effort. Chris just said, "No we are going, we had a long flight and couldn't possibly do the girls justice, we will come again tomorrow." At that, we moved toward the door, the driver followed and we didn't look back, both of us breathed a sigh of relief at their acceptance as we opened the door and walked out to the taxi. We gave the driver, who still had a cigarette in the corner of his mouth, some money and he dropped us off. We had a couple more beers a few doors from where we were staying then back to the hotel to sleep exhausted and still nervously laughing and making jokes, albeit now safely at a distance, about the guy with the revolver.

I had a very disturbed night having odd dreams probably as a result of the flight, the change of environment and cultures, noisy air-conditioning and jetlag and our experiences. After all, we had gone through a host of them completely at odds with what we were used to and were exhausted beyond where we could have imagined.

I kept wakening and going to the toilet after all the beers. Sleepily and still inebriated on this one particular trip, I closed the door behind me and fully opened my eyes to find bright lights and no toilet. All too quickly I began to realise that accidentally I had taken the room door to the corridor instead of the toilet and in my half sleep. I watched in horror as almost in slow motion, the door clicked closed behind me and I was locked out of the room. Frantically I knocked on the door shouted as much as I dare as it was in the early hours and didn't want someone to hear and come out of an adjacent room and see me naked at the door. Chris had had too many beers and didn't hear above the din of the ageing air-conditioning unit. The options in the frantic thinking to eliminate any embarrassment diminished to zero in a split second. Standing stark naked in the bright hallway I would have paid more than the cost of one girl in the hen house for just a pair of underpants. After searching for a linen cupboard that might have been open, I thought it better to quickly get to the reception rather than be caught by other guests, naked in the corridor trying doors. That would take some explaining. How could I have been so stupid as to get myself in such a predicament? I took the stairs down to the ground thinking that people up at that time would be taking the lift to or from their rooms. The night porter was beside himself as I walked into the reception without a stitch of clothing. Without saying a word there was an uncomfortable pause where I could see the thought that went through his head…how the hell could this happen? I hurriedly explained the story struggling with every word as they gave me a blanket from behind the desk. They took it in good humour; it was as if they had other much worse things had happened to guests there. No doubt they had but that was about as bad as I wanted to experience.

We were still less than a couple of days into our world-spanning adventure and still in the short term rest of our lives, but it seemed like a lifetime since we had left home on the train and those first few hours' lamenting of friends. It wasn't the first time we had given in to the lure of adventure for the fun of it. From being young doing mischievous kids' stuff like syphoning petrol from other cars to make our way back from Scotland after the weekend of shooting geese. We lost the cash we had on the Solway and hadn't shot anything to sell. Or poaching pheasants or trout and salmon in the Lake District, we certainly were in the thick of breaking the same daily routine. That poaching was illegal? We had a different way of looking at it. Before the turn of the twentieth century, eight out of ten of the cases put before the crown was for poaching. Since then terrible crimes that are much more heinous have been happening. So our remedy was that people should spend more time poaching, therefore, reducing serious crimes. It worked for us at the time!

We knew that spending this kind of time in these circumstances halfway around the world meant that nothing was ever the same again. Already we felt different. It was a whirlwind of experiences, all this stuff happening as a matter of course, happening around us, no humdrum repetitions of going down to the pub, we had got off to quite a busy and hilarious start, if not a little bit tricky at times. Insouciant empaths educating ourselves with no expectations and no preconceived ideas, fundamentally because we had no idea what was to come. It wasn't so much of a philosophy, we didn't have one, as it was a necessary reality and we were in the throes of it, completely blind but absorbing it all. As the first couple of days had unfolded, so much interaction with all the people we had met, being back at home and those relationships that we had left was a very different concept and so distant from our thinking now. It wasn't that we didn't care, there just wasn't the time or mental space to think about anything else that may be happening elsewhere or happening outside of what we were doing. In the fleeting times that the past life, even though it was after such a short time of being away, came into mind we didn't consider relationships anymore we just went from day to day, taking it in and creating a bit of fun. That's all we thought. As if the past was not forgotten but left on the back burner we would get back to later, however later that would be.

The next day we did the tourist bit and walked around the city and port and had lunch at the Raffles Hotel. We sat for a while to take in the style, history and grandeur of the place but left before the bewitching hour of the g and t afternoon snifter more I think because of the price than the time. We called to check, as agreed on leaving the hotel in the morning if the airline had left a message to find that they had. We had been booked on a flight later that evening and after a short walk back to the hotel we packed and in the early evening went out to the airport. Realising by now, in such alternate surroundings and circumstances with people we didn't have much understanding of, things could go wrong in front of our eyes rapidly. I still had the spine-chilling experience in mind of standing stark naked in the hotel hallway having thought only split seconds before that I knew what I was doing, we guardedly allowed plenty of time to get there and to ensure we got things right. It was still a mystery how the rescheduling of the flights worked. It was somehow a stunning fete that, after things going seriously wrong thousands of miles away with the plane delayed through 'technical problems', and yet could be pulled back together and put back on track to finish the journey remotely. It also made us feel important as they had politely done it all for us. Of course, once this had been sorted out, it was standard procedure that miracles can happen and would be expected forever more but ever since I have had a healthy respect for people's collective ability to organise. There is a skill in making things work, but a far greater talent is needed to put things that have gone astray back together.

We were off on the next leg to Oz. The girls in the hen house would have to wait until the next time we were there, if and when there ever would be one.

Chapter 3
The Long Haul

We checked the bags and went for a beer. The plan worked well, we were relaxed and had a little more time to take in the airport thing, the people milling around looking at the departure boards and trying to find the right desk at which to check in. I was still in awe of the organisation that is needed to make it all work so that everyone finds the right plane and gets to where they want to go. Right first time, no dummy runs, no folks in Moscow not the Maldives with their baggage in Belgium. Fascinating! Neither of us had been in a commercial airliner until this trip. London's Heathrow was all new and a blur with so many new and different things going on but now after that experience, we were able to absorb activity more readily, we knew a bit more about what was happening and understood what people were doing and why. Most youths had been on a package tour or two, maybe at first with their parents and then maybe with a group of friends. We had until then organised our own holiday time mainly involving wholesome country pursuits like shooting and fishing. Most of our holidays were spent in the UK travelling by car because there were plenty of places to go to of interest. Living with Scotland and particularly the Lake District nearby, there was always somewhere different, picturesque and interesting to go. Further, if you packed up and went anywhere in the UK and you didn't like where you were for whatever reason, you could go on to the next place or another you had in mind that might be good. This Norma and I did a lot of and spent several holidays in and around Looe in Cornwall. One time we went to Norfolk and didn't like it so much so the next day we spent driving to Cornwall again where we knew we enjoyed. So it wasn't because we were not adventurous or could not afford to go abroad, we had a good time in the UK, so the idea didn't come to mind with any great desire. Most package tours were only on the continent and not that exotic. Exotic was much further afield and the cost of that sort of trip was out of our reach at the time.

A couple of years before this much more major jaunt I had been through France and Spain and on to Portugal and back by car with friends. Yes, it was different than being back in the UK but although there were the customs and ferry interval to differentiate between countries providing the abroad feeling, it was not so different, not such a jolt to the senses. Houses and countryside although a little different, all pretty much following the same format as the UK. Yes you drove on the other side of the road, yes it was difficult making out what the road signs were but it was still driving and a slow process of going from one place/country to another. The views were similar to the UK with some regional differences but changes almost crept up on you and there was no great jolt to the imagination. Flying, seeing nothing but the inside of the plane, apart from the virtually surreal view out of the window which was almost the same as watching a TV screen, and alighting in a completely alien environment was very different. There was no real sense of having gone anywhere as all we did was to sit on the plane. Yes, we knew we had travelled thousands of miles but there was no real sense of having done so, not until you arrive and look around to nice and feel the degree of difference.

The first part of our epic journey was all so new that simply making sure we did the right thing, going to the right place, drop the bags and gathering ourselves together etc., took up our mental capacity. We did not want to contemplate the consequences of getting it wrong and even less the cash impact of such. The 'what the hell next' scenario as we were watching the plane that we were supposed to be on taking off into the distance was something we didn't want to experience, so all effort went into not having to. Now we were seasoned travellers, or so we were calling ourselves with 10,000 miles or so under our belt, we were already halfway around the world and had made our mark on the international flying staff and community. The stewardesses now were pretty much everyday people and not the high untouchable or unapproachable goddesses we (and our peers) had imagined. "You know, she's a good looking girl, bet she's an air hostess, lucky if you are in with a chance with her." They were now just like the other girls we had been amongst or taken out, nothing completely different or out of reach. Just girls who we had managed to befriend if not impress and who had thoroughly enjoyed our company albeit that at some stages we took them beyond the norm of what they were used to with passengers. They did have fun and I am sure will have remembered and spoken endearingly about us afterwards and some time to come. We had also bounced off some very different cultures and coped, not so easy at first but with a bit of practice enough to communicate with a smattering of humour. Sitting in the airport waiting for the flight call (they did that then) we were relaxed and felt completely on top of things.

There was time too for Chris to mercilessly take the mickey out of me for the experience of finding myself naked in the corridor of the hotel saying that he had heard me knocking on the door and thought he would leave me to sort it out on my own as a survival mission that would make me stronger. Asshole! It did and I would try to help him out in the same way someday. We laughed again as we were finishing our drinks at the bar with the barman chuckling after having eavesdropped the conversation and picking up on the joke. He didn't believe it had happened, we laughed again because we knew it had! Suddenly our flight was called and it was our turn to move along as others dropping in and out of the conversation at the bar had for the last hour or so and we followed the signs and managed to find the right gate.

In Heathrow, leaving the UK, everything was enclosed corridors and walkways which didn't allow any looking around while getting to and on the plane. What you saw was the space you were in of about five by 5 meters space of corridor getting smaller as you neared the plane which you never even saw its exterior and an appreciation of its shape and general appearance, all you saw was its entrance door. It was almost as if it was made that way because you were not supposed to see anything, it was official and as such restricted. Here, as we followed the signs through the open spaces of Changi, we arrived in a huge hall. In front of us there were massive glass doors the whole width of the hall some 40 or 50 meters, three storeys high and just outside them was this gigantic aeroplane in the open air. We both stood there with our mouths open and it took several seconds to take it in. Just when we thought we had travelled enough to see it all, or not far short, we were speechless with the sheer size and spectacle of this plane, humbled again. It was as if it must have arrived from a different world in another galaxy, right at that point, we would have believed it had too. Still struggling to get past the hangover, mellowed slightly by 'hairs of the dog' at the bar, still chuckling about my hotel exposure from the night before, we were fighting to grasp this new reality. Only a couple of days ago our reality didn't stretch beyond the local bars, the ancient stocks and whipping post in the village square of our past lives in our native Poulton. This new reality was positively electric…and happening to us there and then.

People were entering the plane from five or six different stairways along the fuselage that we could see. In the dark, it had become night since entering the airport, the massive glass doors were open letting in the heavy, humid air. The ever-present Asian cackle around us interspersed with the hailing systems announcements. The external floodlights reflected off the damp tarmac and the plane creating an eerie and surreal spectacle. We thought that we had walked into the film set of a science fiction movie. We were both expecting a famous actor to appear along with cameras and crew etc. None of this could be true. The last plane we were on for the first leg of the journey from the UK to Singapore now appeared to be only one-tenth of the size of this one and we thought then that was huge. Nothing that big could move on the ground more than a few yards and even then must have to be towed by a truck or something let alone move fast enough on its own to take-off and fly…impossible!

Eventually, we boarded and sat in total disbelief. We were wide-eyed in awe of the size, two walkways, 11 seats from side to side. It was a brand new, it smelled brand new, Qantas 747 jumbo jet in all its magnificence. How on earth could anybody afford to buy such an item of awesome beauty and thoughtfulness, have strangers fly it and then fill it with people they didn't know? The thought of something so big being incapable of flying subsided with the sight of the two attractive stewardesses making their way along the aisle in their light red skirt suits just above the knee with little red beret-type hats helping people into their seats, a lovely sight. One smile from the frizzy-haired redhead eased the anxiety but not quite wholly. We were still in a state of not knowing with any surety that this next bit was going to work. It eased a little as the thought crossed my mind that no one (I am guessing a man) in their right minds would design and make such a device, put such a desirable young thing inside, that was not going to perform as it should. No one would allow her and several other cute girls to perish, never mind about the passenger's wellbeing. We settled in as they closed up the doors, put everything and everyone in their places, did their pre-flight safety demonstration and the plane taxied to the runway. We felt humbled again by the sheer enormity of world organisation and human achievement to make such a vehicle and make it work properly. If this ever got off the ground, we would be invincible in the skies. No one I ever knew had heard of their existence let alone been in one and related the story, it was exciting and in a way unnerving at the same time.

The plane's engines screamed deafeningly and we rolled along the runway accelerating just as the 707 did (the 707 of that time was a cavalier type character aeroplane, smallish and a bit flash). This time the 747, however, was taking a lot longer with a much deeper roar; this was a far more serious vehicle. It seemed ok at first, but after a while, I started to get the idea that maybe it wasn't going to make it. As we were not off the ground yet the words of the stewardess came back to mind, maybe this was one of those 'technical problems' on take-off in the making! Terrified, further and further it sped along the ground, by now convinced that we were going into the sea at the end of the runway, I could feel an involuntary scream rumbling in the background, how I kept it back, I'll never know. I might have screamed but don't want to remember. I couldn't grasp why all the other passengers were not the same. I didn't dare look at Chris in case seeing my abject horror would push him over the edge; I knew he was petrified as he hadn't spoken at all which was way out of the ordinary for him. At what seemed like two hours past my estimation of when we should be airborne, evidenced by the finger imprints in the armrests, the nose turned up and a second or two later the rear undercarriage lifted to rid us of the vibration and with great relief we were in the sky. Phew! Both of us were white with fear which thankfully subsided at another fleeting glance of the redhead. Another memorable first (albeit that we might have been ok without the horror), next time at least I will not be so impatient with the plane manufacturers' skills and the pilot's abilities…I hope. It's odd what you think about in times of riveting, abject stress. For a split second at the very point we took off I remembered the Einstein quote where a friend asked him to explain his theory of relativity, which baffled me and everyone else I expect. He pondered a moment and in his remarkable genius, also a humanist and comedian he said, 'It's like talking to a beautiful girl for two hours and thinking it was two minutes or sitting on a hot stove for two minutes and thinking it was two hours'. All blokes have experienced the first part, now I knew the downside to the second part and understood his simile thoroughly.

As it was evening time, we ate and slept after a little banter with the girls until woken by the effects of severe turbulence over the northern coastline of Australia. Drinks spilt and people rushed back to their seats swaying from one side of the walkways to the other banging into the seats, stewardesses ushering others back to their seats as the severe shaking went on for several minutes. They said it was unusually violent, the plane gave another loud crack each time it buffeted. I look out of the window to see the wings and engines waving around as if they were only fastened loosely waiting to be fixed properly to the body of the plane. It was not so disconcerting to me but Chris was ashen again. His mood changed and he didn't say anything for quite some time which again was very rare for him. Again I tried to explain a few principles but he didn't want to talk, occupied with getting over it, he was silent.

Albeit not on such a grand scale, in an RAF Chipmunk trainer I had several flying lessons from my Air Training Corps days. The first was at the tender age of 13. I had been singled out for the one slot for one hour that was available from Squires Gate airport just outside of my hometown as I had just been promoted and it was a perk of the new rank. On the day they led me out to the plane almost crouched, as was the method then with the parachute as a base to sit on in the plane, watched over by a young RAF pilot officer. I sat in the steel bucket seat cushioned by the parachute as we trundled over the grass; I can remember thinking that we must be getting close to the runway soon for take-off when suddenly we were up in the air. I was foxed before we had started. Over the radio he asked me if I had flown before, being young and daft I told him, sure I had, many times. If I only knew at that time how big a mistake I'd made I wouldn't have been so quick to appear smart boasting like a fool. "Okay," he says, from his voice firmly convinced that I was talking a load of tripe, "let's do some aerobatics."

"Great," I say without a clue as to what was going to happen.

"First we'll do what we call a stall turn." I nod and grunt like a seasoned grown up wondering what the hell he meant but making a few guesses. Stall turn, could have meant anything, a joke or something. We're going to turn! Oh no we're not, sort of thing. The plane went into a steep climb; I found that I couldn't lift my arms from the edges of the seat until we apparently got to the top of the climb where the plane hung in mid-air (the stall) on the propeller and then we peeled off (the turn) sideways. All this time it was impossible for me to hold my arms down, my stomach was still at the turn a couple of hundred meters in the sky as we plummeted down towards the earth which seemed without the engine running. Filled with horror, I didn't know whether that was planned or not of course. It certainly wasn't that joke, we're going to do it, no we're not. We'd done it! A split second from the ground, I had already the picture of the fire crew and ambulances arriving on the crash scene as the pilot and I were dying in the burning wreckage, the engine fired and I thought my arms and whole body come to that, would drop through the underside of the plane, as he in my imagination, was fighting for both our lives to level it out without hitting the ground. We started to climb again. By this time chilled with fear and the inexplicable changes in pressure and altitude, I couldn't hear a thing, my ears had not equalised. Thank the lord for that, I'm not dead. At that point, I imagined myself on the ground watching this (probably though wishing I was there) and thinking how horrifying it would be merely watching it happen let alone what it would be like in the plane. It must have been my complete denial defence system kicking in spiriting my body anywhere else than in the sky in that plane.

He hadn't finished there, in fact little did I know, he had hardly started. We climbed further and steeper, my arms again riveted to the seat and levelled. In the background I vaguely heard him say barrel something. Suddenly my arms were once again uncontrollably up in the air and I lost equilibrium altogether, thinking what it was that had changed? I looked for the sky but that had gone completely, then it appeared again on the opposite side to where it disappeared. Bang went my equilibrium again. We levelled off and again went through another 360-degree roll. By then we were over the North Sea and near the Isle of Mann. Just as I was gaining some orientation and about to take in the scenery we went into a steep climb as he was saying "now a loop". By this time I had completely given in to the fact that I had no idea, what was happening, where I was, whether I was up or down or what was next and had no control of anything headspace at all. I was coping this time however with the forces on my arms but as we got to the top, instead of peeling off to the side, we kept on going over. Arms up, arms down, sky, sea, land all was completely jumbled along with my equilibrium once more until after several minutes of level flight. "Let's just try that one again." I made out of some muffled words over the radio, my ears still not working properly when over in a loop we went again. By that stage (as my father used to say) I didn't know whether it was New Year or New York. As we levelled out again, I could just make out the Fleetwood coast and he asked if there was anywhere I would like to go. I said something which I thought unintelligible and we flew lower over my home village and went back to the airfield. I still couldn't hear properly and still completely disorientated as they levered me out of the back of the plane. Thank goodness I wasn't sick, or even worse. The pilot, who couldn't have been more the 19 or 20 years old said, "A little tip for the future in life, never tell anyone that you are more experienced than you really are." I tried to tell him something but my head still couldn't string the words together and get them to my mouth properly. Another assistant guy helped me back to the building and that was that. I sat in the airport for a while until I felt almost like I was before we had taken off. I flew several times after that but took his advice, learned and enjoyed every minute. It was a landmark memory, although not in every case from then on whenever having a choice where there were consequences, even if the truth didn't help me any, I tended to stick with relating an actual account of my knowledge and experience rather than exaggerating, just to sound good. Now I knew you could be caught out pretty severely.

The turbulence on the 747 after this experience didn't bother me so much. Chris stayed quiet for some time. The flight time was 10 hours as we ate and drank along with some conversation with the stewardesses and other passengers. Very soon we were making our approach to Melbourne where we never left the plane as it then went on to Sydney. There we boarded a flight to Perth. It was full of people going the other way back to England as Perth was the first call before the Far East. As we were now on a domestic flight, for us that was, we thought we had missed the chance to buy some duty-free cigarettes. When they came round selling them, we told the stewardess no because we thought we would have trouble at Perth airport. She said don't be silly you are taking a domestic flight and checked into Australia in Sydney, you won't have to go through customs or immigration, you can have as much as you like. Thinking about it she could have told us anything to make a sale and we could have been in trouble on our first day in a new country but she was pretty and had a nice smile, we would have believed anything she said, and did. We loaded up with several boxes each.

We collected our luggage and sailed through customs and immigration without a thought except that with the cigs we had swum the channel. A guy was waiting for us in the airport lounge. His job was to take us to a hotel and once there came the blow. We had just one week to find a job and somewhere to stay, after that the hotel would be a cost to us. I don't know just exactly what we expected but I remember thinking from memory that we did expect a little more than the time he gave us. Undeterred, after having steak with an egg on for breakfast we went into the town to find the employment agency for a job. Reality had set in.

Chapter 4
Being There

Earlier, on the flight from Singapore, we were sat next to a coloured guy from South Africa, Ronnie. He was in awe of the exchanges we had with the crew and other people as we treated them alike. We laughed and joked with them, he winced each time we were cheeky to the stewardesses but quietly listened with admiration. He was a mixed breed, father coloured S African Indian and his mother from Pakistan. Chris pressed his buttons about apartheid and slowly wound him up to give us the whole story. His father was a trade union activist that had been in several skirmishes with companies, police and politicians. Coloureds at that time were considered to have less standing than black people, we couldn't help wondering why his father couldn't have picked a less volatile vocation rather than politicking for the rights of coloured workers. Despite all that, from Ronnie's account, he was a very intelligent man. We were sure that life was cheap in South Africa and less than a month's wages would have guaranteed that he wouldn't be seen again without a trace. We could see that Ronnie was a little tough in his thinking and no doubt his father was the source of some of his fire. At the same time, he was able to be humble, a genuine humble. We could also see that in some ways he was very naïve. Maybe that was his way of dealing with the outrageous circumstances that coloured people had to suffer through that time we thought. He had the affliction of rampant social climbing no doubt from the caste system back in his folk's days fired by the environmental and social prejudices of South Africa. You could sense him bragging about his abilities when from the rest of his character that he had already shown us, he was enough of a person anyway. He spoilt himself through exaggerating. Perhaps this was a result of being oppressed. It turned out that he was older than us by a few years. We had thought he was younger because of his attitude and demeanour. We did have a bit of a problem believing some of his stories after we had seen this in his character. He had already spent some time in Oz and had a job as a welder working for a metal furniture company not far from his house. We started to feel the Aussie prejudices coming from him that he had obviously picked up from the locals. We just brushed it off as him trying to gain some credence and easing his insecurities from his treatment in S Africa. Generally, people in these circumstances do have their prejudices but because of the racial prejudices they have to suffer, they hide their own because they know it to be wrong, by voicing those attitudes picked up from others. We later discovered that he suffered from severe jealousy too which must have made its hell in some corner of his mind that also governed some of the things he did and said. Overall, although messed up from some of his not so nice experiences, he wasn't such a bad lad and appreciated some of our British humour enough to have him rolling into the aisle once or twice before we left the plane in Sydney for him to take some other connection over to Perth.

The father had been through some sort of ordeal, of which it seemed he had many and was at present in India. He had been to Australia some months earlier and bought a house in Bicton, a little town off the freeway between Perth and Freemantle. As Perth was our final destination (why Perth, still neither of us could remember we just said we must have had a reason at some point) we said we would look him up once we got there, so he gave us his address and telephone. He'd said that if we were stuck for somewhere to sleep for a night or two, we could stay at his place while we were looking for an apartment, as he was on his own until his father and later the rest of his family could make the trip. We thought no more of it at the time because first, we were ok for accommodation as we had been assured of a long period in a hotel until we found jobs where after we could afford our own place. Secondly, we were told that there were plenty of jobs to be had. We could take a driving job or something else to get on our feet until something with better prospects came along. After a couple of days visiting the employment office without any prospect of a job (at which we were stunned), we decided to look him up. Slightly bruised as we thought there would be stacks of jobs as the emigration people had told us but literally, nothing, not one job offered on this the first pass or at several others after.

--oo--

The bus stopped on the freeway and we walked for some way along it before we found the street on which his house was. As I swatted the flies from out of my eyes and ears and the corners my mouth, I could hear Chris cursing. A friend from back home had said of our trip, "What do you want to go there for, sand sore eyes and bastard flies?" How right he was. They were so persistent, no bites (although some did) and just a continual and confounded nuisance. Hardly a reason not to go to Oz but after a while of the same one (or so it seemed) coming back six or seven times to the same spot and encouraging others to do the same, you were absolutely in no doubt whatever why someone coined the phrase. Chris chirps up, "Millions of them killed every hour of the day and they still don't know why we take every chance to swat them. Evolution didn't hand them such a good package for development and longevity."

"Since when were you a scientist?" I say.

"Since one of the daft bastard flew in my mouth and I swallowed it," he replies, "that's exactly what I mean, you don't see many flies as scientists do you? I'd rather have wasps, at least they don't spit on your food!"

"You don't see many wasps as scientists either," I say.

"Thar ya gao *brerce*," says Chris with an Oz accent, "nor dentists cobber! That would be something you could make money out of, training flies for dentistry, a team of them flying around your mouth with drills and stuff."

"We don't even know how to do it so how can we teach them?"

"Yes," he says, "but the flies don't know that!" It wasn't just the flies but the sun also getting to our heads as we started ducking to avoid an unwanted extraction or filling. We were more delirious than we thought maybe because of the heat. Street dentistry, by his time we were in tears laughing and hoping no one would see us. "It's like the joke, the dentist has his surgery in an American sports car, he calls it Transam dental medication."

"Who told you that?" says Chris.

"A young Portuguese lad in a caravan on a campsite just outside of Lisbon," I say.

Chris was flabbergasted; he admired the quality of diverse bullshit in return and replies, "Careful, with those kinds of stories I'm going to start calling you Ronnie." The funny bit was that the guy in a caravan in Lisbon was true, which made it even more hilarious.

The frivolities had passed some of the time as we were walking, as it always had over the last weeks, but somehow we managed to remember the quest of getting to Ronnie's house and by some miracle by this time we were in the right street. Neither of us remembered thinking about or specifically looking for it. It certainly wasn't through Chris's directional prowess. All single storey houses and most of them timber built and most standing a meter or so off the ground. We didn't realise at the time but this was to try to ward off some of the noxious insects there are in Oz, of which there are many. By far the majority of mosquitoes stay within a meter of the earth, so it reduces the number of bites you get if you are higher up. The rest of the spiders and scorpions and snakes or whatever other fearsome crawlies don't find it as easy to get inside as just slithering through the grass and into a doorway at ground level. I guess all in all, not a bad idea. You can't help but relate things back to what you would expect to see back in Blighty and this area and style reminded me a little of the UK. There are areas by rivers and creeks in tidal areas where there were many similar buildings. Most of them timber built and without proper planning consent, each with a considerable amount of land around them. The land was not at a premium here and no fear of over-population. Most had red, green or cream tiled roofs, if not corrugated asbestos type panels and I couldn't help thinking again just how much it was similar to the UK. After the stop-off in Singapore where everything was Asian, it was unique to find something that could well have been in an outlying rural area of the UK, but here we were over 10,000 miles away. We looked at the numbers and judging by the size of most of the plots and as we were some 100 or more numbers away from the number Ronnie had given us, we still had a fair walk ahead.

It was the equivalent of a good-sized country lane if basing it on UK standards, deadly straight and flat almost as far as you could see, with the houses sparsely dotted on each side. It gave the idea of space and distance and almost implied loneliness in being remote and sparsely populated. Unlike the UK the glaring difference here was that there were pavements on both sides. I have never been since but it was a very nice and peaceful area. No doubt now it will be built up with expensive houses if not blocks of apartments being in a prime location on the outskirts of both Perth and Freemantle. But right now not so smart as some of the buildings were derelict. As we were walking, we remembered Ronnie and his tallish stories and started to imagine that maybe there wasn't a house at all but a little broken down shanty town shack with no roof and no better than sleeping in the open air (a few we passed had roofs caved in). How was he going to deal with that when we turned up on his doorstep?

Suddenly we were there, outside the number several hundred and something. It didn't look as bad as we had jokingly imagined. In need of a grass cut, some maintenance and a coat of paint but not so bad. A similar style on stilts as the others we had passed. We started to feel guilty about doubting what Ronnie told us and thought it might be a ram shackled building; it was pretty much as he had described when we met on the plane.

Ronnie came to the door and smiled when he saw us, he seemed a bit uneasy for some reason. Nothing serious, in fact, after it sunk in that we were there, in ways he appeared pleased to see us. He said that he never expected to see us again which we found odd for him to say. Then it dawned, I began to see him in a different light. He was older than we were but it was now very apparent his mental age was considerably less. Albeit that we were younger, he looked up to us. It seemed weird because he did not immediately look older than us and his immature demeanour didn't give this away either. From the conversation on the plane, it was going to be a while before his father turned up and I think he was hoping that we would come to stay in the house as a bit of security and company for him. We sat and talked for a while and he said we should come and stay. It was like winning the pools after the last couple of days of disappointments we'd had. We settled on the idea that we would work out some rent for the room when his father arrived. There was no hurry as he didn't have rent to pay and we were good company, absolutely almost too good to be true.

The house was quite spacious. Three bedrooms, a bathroom and a small kitchen and a dining room and lounge together. The entrance was in the middle of the front flank and through it, you were in the hall of more than two meters wide which gave it a palatial touch. To the right the lounge and diner with the small kitchen at the rear. On the left were the three bedrooms with the bathroom straight ahead. At the front a lawn with a middle pathway to the five or so steps that led to the entrance door. Some space on both sides of the building about the width of a driveway. To have such space in the UK would be a luxury compared to the terraces or semi-detached houses that was the norm. To the rear a large grassy area about twenty meters deep. It was very pleasant and would make a nice, spacious family home.

Ronnie went to work each day which left Chris and I hanging around twiddling our thumbs. No rush now to find work to pay rent as we were not paying any. We were bored and after trips to the employment office and literally, nothing had come our way. We thought there must be a job driving or something similar but we were offered nothing. We then took jobs selling encyclopaedias and sold a couple but it was a rotten task which neither of us fitted into or enjoyed, trudging around residential areas in the hot sun. We met an English guy who had been good at it and earned well. So good he bought himself a new MGB roadster, he and his pregnant girlfriend soon to be wife went on a trip through the outback. One day with the roof down and not a care in the world speeding along through the outback, as you would on an open road with no restrictions and that sort of car, they hit a rogue kangaroo. This almost 100 kilo one and a half meter animal leapt from the side of the road, landed on the bonnet and then, this weight combined with their momentum at 50 or 60 miles per hour bowled straight through the windscreen and crushed his girlfriend. She and the baby were killed outright and quite understandably he was distraught and in the hospital for weeks. The car was a totalled. We were spellbound listening to the story which took a horrifying turn, out of the blue, that was the last thing we would have anticipated. It took all his physical strength and will to get his head back together and working again. He was still in the healing some of the wounds when we met. He was a nice guy still in trauma over the death of the girl and child and wiped out financially with still some medical bills outstanding. He had gone from the top of the world as an ace salesman without a care, about to be married and have a family, to the absolute depths of despair. The story knocked strength out of us too, it was such a vivid tale of woe. Coupled with our dislike of the job and not being very good at it we left, wondering what we should do next.

Ronnie came back from work one day saying that he had mentioned us to the foreman at work. They were looking for staff and as his father would soon be here it would be better if we were earning to pay some rent, perhaps we should go along. The next day we saw the foreman. They needed a welder and a press operator which we managed to fast chat ourselves into the jobs. I had used welding equipment before so it came back to me, slowly. Chris had no clue what he was doing but managed to hold the job down bored to tears.

The factory was huge, about a hundred and fifty metres or more long. Chris got to know every inch of it as, not doing too well on the press through abject boredom, they made him sweep up the 25 or so metres wide causeway all round it. It took days in the hot sunshine. The factory was in a wooded cul-de-sac about 30 minutes' walk from the house, quite a pleasant trip each morning and good exercise. It was an area where budgerigars and parrots gathered, like starlings do in the UK but these were there every day, it was where they lived. There were thousands of them and consequently there were always many of them on the floor that had died, through natural causes I would guess. The chirping noise of those high in the trees enjoying life was deafening as we walked beneath them each morning. As a child, we had a family budgerigar. For no apparent reason, it had food and water and a fairly big cage, it would continually chirp, a loud shrill chirp that would hurt your ears but for hours on end like it was angry at something. We had to cover the cage to try and calm it and even then it seemed forever before the bird would calm down and the din would stop. Having thousands of them doing the same thing was just too much to contemplate for a long period. It was a pleasure to get inside the factory and work. Well, that was my justification for going inside the place each morning to a not so salubrious job welding in 100 degrees in a factory without air-conditioning. We had to eat salt tablets each day to replace what had left in the gallons of sweat.

--oo--

After a few weeks of this daily routine of sleeping, a few beers in the evenings and walking to the factory in the mornings Ronnie's father Ravi finally arrived. It changed the atmosphere in the house from a lads retreat to more of a family home. He went to great lengths to establish this in preparation for his wife and Ronnie's sister to arrive. From the first day, both of us had some respect for Ravi and he was interesting and played some cards, close to his chest in more ways than one. As it happened, he was very slick at Bridge. There were many inferences in his method and tone while we spoke which we would ponder for some time. We agreed to rent and had the one room of the three that were available. The deal included food as Ravi was a hotshot in the kitchen. The diet was simple, lamb, lamb and lamb. We had every type of lamb curry you could imagine and although a bit monotonous after a while, he was pretty good at it. After a month of the same, when we asked if he could vary the dishes a little, he looked at us as if we were crazy. We didn't ask again.

He had picked up on how much influence we were in Ronnie's thinking. Having spent many hours in the evenings chatting together, in our openness and carefree attitude he had learned a lot about being a lad rather than his father's influence that purely made him into young adult along with all the responsibility of a trade union activist father. Yes ok, there was a lot that Ronnie should be grateful for from his father's efforts but Ronnie had his own life and his natural wants and desires as to how life should be. We enjoyed sporting with his dad on this level and helping Ronnie be an individual rather than solely an image of his father. It was paradoxical that, in his father's attempt to make him more grown up, he ended up younger than his years, Ravi knew the effect because he defended the fact. Ravi didn't appreciate this so much and made a conscious effort to win him back and was embarrassed in some instances where Ronnie repeated something we had said and known the wisdom but felt he had to disagree. Ronnie, of course, was still his son but we did make an impression on him and I'm sure we had an effect on him for the rest of his life. Our thinking was quite obtuse to his narrowed vision of the world brought about by his upbringing and circumstances. Ravi, through all his perception and own prejudices, couldn't help but appreciate and condone some of those influences. It was interesting to see in Ronnie, he started growing up in front of us which was to a greater or lesser degree uncomfortable for Ravi.

Ravi always had in mind his wife, Ronnie's mother arriving which was supposed to be imminent. After some conversations with Ronnie on the way to the factory in the mornings, that wasn't an absolute foregone conclusion that she was coming. There were delays from the original dates of her arrival. He didn't tell us the whole story, we thought because he didn't know it fully from her but there was some reluctance on her part to leave S Africa. From the bits Ronnie didn't tell us, we started to understand that his father was in greater trouble that he had led us to believe. It would seem that she had disagreed with much of his politics and method and now not as supportive of his cause as it had brought much trouble into their lives as the resultant aftermath that he was dealing proved. Although she was dependent on him, her life and circle of people seemed threatened by the nature of his work. It was easy to see they had major issues. We were not 100% sure but all the facts seemed to the point that way. From the conversation, although not actually said, it also seemed that their troubles had brought them close to a more permanent separation, something Ronnie was struggling with this concept and nervous as to the eventual outcome.

It appeared that this was what was being played out in the background to cause the delays and indecision. It was confusing to us to think about it to help Ronnie, which usually means that you are missing something. When things don't add up, it's generally because the truth was not included in the equation. We didn't condemn him for not being straight as he was doing as much as he could to explain, the whole backdrop of subversion from where he was coming didn't allow him to be truthful. It was a shame because I had gone through the breakup of parents; not saying that that was where Ravi and his wife were going but I had some thinking that would have been useful to him, if that was the arena of the parents thinking. Maybe a few dos and don'ts as to what he should or shouldn't involve himself in their wrangling's. The troubles with Ravi's work could have been a mask for deeper troubles in their relationship. Anyway we tried to help with the information he was willing to part with and he appreciated us for the effort.

While she was deciding and making plans to come, life went on for us in much the same routine. We played Bridge many nights and Ravi would tell us stories about where basic human rights didn't matter and whoever disagreed were beaten or just simply disappeared. At one stage with a case he was fighting regarding deaths and injuries in a mining accident he was charged with offences of some kind and had to spend some time in India while a way around or over the accusations was sought. It seemed continuous in his life in South Africa, he would go from one confrontation to another each time coming up against the injustices of apartheid and the knock-on effects for the everyday coloured and black population. You could see that he had a lot more to tell, much more graphic detail of experiences that he decided to keep to himself.

Ronnie's mother arrived and a lot of our notions were confirmed. It was interesting watching the relationships between them pan out. They had a family bond between them but were very disturbed influences which subconsciously we put down almost wholly to the injustices that they suffered. It was also clear that there were many frictions between her and Ravi. He was a very intelligent man, he knew what we were doing with Ronnie, nothing sinister as we were just who we were and in a lot of ways showed we sympathised. However, the selfish ego merry-go-round that was inevitably contagious in such a social situation from where they came from kept appearing. It was sad to see. We all do it to a degree, where you have fundamentally good people caught up in such oppressive surroundings. Instead of remaining detached the tendency is to compete with it. It's doubly sad and destructive to their quest of being free from such as by default they are making the outside stuff they were vehemently against acceptable. To avoid being too involved or sad about it, we would look to find an amusing angle which we usually managed to find. Two happy-go-lucky irresponsible people like us could see this folly and were a godsend, not subjected to the same, Ronnie picked up on these moments like a child with a bag of sweets albeit a little guardedly in praise of us through respect for his father. Chris and I were soaking up the education. Seeing this happen and not being involved in the same, made it not so much hard work or a drudgery contemplating it on their behalf. Looking back, it was brave of us to try to help but at that time, both Ronnie and his father had a healthy respect for us which showed through them feeling secure enough to open themselves up into talking to us.

This principle was made more crystal clear to all when Ronnie in his openness would say something we had made clear to him. He would confirm the good attitude and independent views we brought to the household. Ravi may criticise something Chris or I said, and Ronnie would defend us from a moral standpoint. Ravi tried to defend his or his wife's' opinion but couldn't without displaying some of the very prejudicial behaviours that they abhorred. Chris and I would pick up on this in a flash and laugh highlighting the irony as they argued themselves to a standstill. They took it in good heart most of the time. More often than not everyone got it as we mercilessly drove home the point, often all laughed uncontrollably. Job done, thought Chris and me.....but not every time alas. Although entertained and dare say enlightened, it was mostly the mother that felt a bit short-changed after one of these events. Maybe she just felt outnumbered, or maybe it was just the female thing of not feeling completely in control irrespective of how right we were. We would get to a stage in thinking where we knew it wasn't constructive to dig any deeper with her. She had her demons, of a female variety which were relevant only to her, outside of our male mental framework. Not outside of our understanding but something we didn't need to involve ourselves with.

You know when you meet people for the first time you miss some of the things they say. Everything that people think and say is important to them but on a first meeting, both parties are dealing with their own thoughts as well as dealing with those exchanges and the conversation topics. Things are said that aren't picked up by the other. Not always because you are not listening but because whatever was said, you consider irrelevant or a distraction to the topic in debate at that time. Sometimes you take no notice because, from your experience of that topic or situation, you know what the person says is not the avenue to pursue. Having considered it previously and applied much constructive thought and know what they say goes nowhere and isn't helpful. It is irrelevant, you don't even note it like a turning in the road that isn't your turning. It's not the only reason why don't respond to every comment but just one of them in this example. It's like when you ask someone what the opposite of love is, instinctively they say hate. You just say no it isn't, the opposite of love is ignorance. To try and explain why to someone at the time would be superfluous because it isn't until you have thought about it that it will make sense. Explaining your equations and calculations which make you arrive at that conclusion if you could or even wanted to, will not benefit them at all. It's something they have to think through themselves and reach their own conclusions. It has to be their thinking and the use of their intellect for it to have meaning. They cannot import your meaning and claim it as theirs, if they do, it will never be real to them.

Several of these moments happened to us as Ronnie did a lot of the talking (unusual with Chris and me around) during our first meeting on the plane. So much of peoples' lives are spent arguing things that don't make any difference to them at all and especially with those who are oppressed in some way. It didn't mean that he was stupid and we didn't make him think that he was (except maybe in jest to highlight a point we would like to think), it was interesting just listening and finding out what he thought and why. Maybe he never had anyone listen to him properly before that he trusted enough to open up. We lifted him from his depressed state, from him leaving his family in whatever disagreeable circumstances they were in and didn't treat him oppressively. Back then on the plane when he left us, he didn't think he would ever see us again. Because we were streets ahead of him in his thinking and he knew it, he thought he was lucky to have met us. He didn't think he had anything to offer us at all and it was him taking from us. That was the reason for his comment at the door, maybe he had reflected on what we said and was embarrassed by the way he was with us, maybe?

His racist background influenced him, on the other hand, we didn't have to think about that stuff at all so none of the arguments he was involved in had any relevance to us. That was why he enjoyed our company. The other aspect was that we seemed to change his thinking fundamentally. The oppression forces people into a mental conflict of dealing with the effects and symptoms of the problem away from the core issue and the problem itself. It's a trick of the oppressor. He didn't know it but we learned a lot about ourselves from that first meeting as well as he. In a completely different groove of course, as a minimum, it confirmed to us the value of our background. The big lesson for us was the degree to which we were not 'fucked up'. Carefree to the point of being irresponsible, which some could construe as being 'fucked up'. At least we were 'fucked up' in a carefree way. We didn't have the traits born from the denial of rights and fundamental immoral restrictions they had faced and didn't give a tinker's toss for anyone trying to impose such. Once Ronnie had got that idea he was sincerely respectful which demonstrated his appreciation. That's why it was a pleasure, for the majority of occasions, to have these debate sessions often whilst we were playing cards. That's probably why Ravi always won; maybe he encouraged the debates so that we lost concentration on the game. Sneaky!

For Ronnie's benefit, instead of his father being threatened by us, he should have encouraged us more. The trouble was that some of the principles Ronnie was struggling with, Ravi either didn't know or had forgotten. The frustration, anger and hatred through oppression blinded him from actually expediting and allowing the very principles he was supposedly fighting to establish. But of course, now in the home environment, Ravi did feel threatened by our influence, Ronnie was substituting one authority for another...which wasn't his. His authority over Ronnie was also made up of and within their oppressed experience. We didn't have one thought of any authority on this issue; we just thought what we thought...and didn't have anyone tell us what to think, that was the choice we had. With us around, Ronnie was now seeing life from a different perspective, not one of injustice because his free will was being oppressed. That was an added sadness to the dilemma which his father had to deal with. Although he and we liked to see Ronnie assert himself, both of them through their own indoctrination couldn't help their prejudices, innate or inherited. In asserting themselves they paradoxically slipped into the same way that they, themselves, had been oppressed. We, on the other hand, didn't really mind what they did or thought, it didn't make any difference to us at all as we knew better from living more free lives. We just were just the relatively none oppressed people we were, we knew what was right and got on with it no matter what or how other people's prejudices guided them to where they were. The main difference was that we didn't have to prove who we were. If we influenced him/them, fine. If they chose to do or be or say something different, that was fine too. It didn't make us feel uncomfortable or lacking in any way. We all have our hang-ups if that's the best description, but we didn't have to be aggressive with them to force an issue or put across a point because that's not how we were taught to deal with those issues. Some nights we would lie in bed hurting with laughter at how ridiculous the debates got. For good or for bad at that time in our situation, we would laugh because that's all we could do in the face of the conundrums that arose. The fact was, they had gotten so used to their circumstances, it was normal, a kind of national or racial Stockholm syndrome. That takes some sorting out. No wonder there are disturbing social problems under these circumstances, troubles arise where the causes are so deeply rooted and confused (on purpose where education is not available and encouraged), that no one knows how or why they started. We went so far but decided that laughter was better than anger and frustration because after all, it wasn't our problem thank goodness.

Altogether it was a good experience for all and we took from it nothing more than the others were willing to give, albeit there were times when they particularly felt uncomfortable. We gave the points of view and attitudes and it was up to them to adopt them…...or not. We didn't come from that same background and from what we could gather from our upbringing, oppression doesn't work ultimately. If anything we were rebellious and knew we could get away with it. If they were rebellious rather than being able to laugh it off, it was almost fatal, they would most likely be shot or jailed or beaten so a lot of their disapproval had to be kept inside to materialise in all manner of odd ways later along the line. We were, excepting marriage and sex etc., (in which Ronnie was also underdeveloped displaying embarrassment whenever the topic arose) that I hope he eventually became involved in, the best thing that happened to Ronnie.

Dictatorships want to suppress education, along with a large spoon of religion, folk are much easier to control. Our background was one of having a compulsory education as all kids do in the UK and most other western countries. Importantly, where Ronnie was educated, they were still involved in this despotic stuff. We just disagreed with whatever didn't stack with us. Our radical views, although not radical to us were far too radical for them to adapt themselves wholly in their other lives. It worked out fine and although Ravi used to beat us at Bridge every game, we didn't mind so much. That was his game, didn't involve any of us getting arrested for what we believed and that suited us all. The introduction of Ronnie's mother changed that balance a bit, she played a good Bridge game but now there was five, pairing became difficult with the relationships. There were problems with Ronnie and his mum playing his dad with one of us. Or the other way around where one of us was paired with his mum or dad, even worse so card playing took a back seat or we went back to playing the original four. Any arguments about these combinations were of immature jealousies and nothing to do with how fair the choices of partners were.

-oo-

We made a few friends at work. Another Englishman, a welder from Nottingham called Peter. He was a bit off beam. He had a spiders web tattoo centred on each elbow and blond hair beyond shoulder length held back in a band. We called him Cochise. We would go to a couple of local beach bars mostly during the day on Saturday or Sunday and have the jug of beer in the middle of the table. Sometimes we had barbecues at his place. Even though he was a friend of Ronnie too, he would never come with us sighting that it was an opportunity to spend time with his folks. We never entertained at Ronnie's either, he didn't think it would work. Cochise had a sister also girlfriend he was trying to offload as he had found another. His mum was single and quite nice too. The now out of favour girlfriend was a bit sweet on me, handy for Cochise, and likewise the sister on Chris. We helped out as much as we could. An evening with Cochise and his family who enjoyed our company was a welcome change from the evenings with Ronnie's family.

Overall though, we were not going anywhere with what we were doing. We didn't have the circles of people that might have provided a route to getting anywhere. The only way of changing was to get another job and move nearer into the city centre to expand the contacts we had but as for looking for another job, there wasn't anything. Generally, the opportunities in Australia were rarer than earlier expectations of people travelling there because of the financial downturn. Life, although we had some fun, wasn't as easy or as fruitful as we imagined and we started to think of maybe returning to the UK. It was part of the plan in leaving England that we should take the trip back overland. Not quite so quickly as we were now imagining but one of the ideas that appealed in travelling halfway around the world was that we should come back via the Far East and India etc.

We started looking at the possibilities. We looked at flights and boat trips and decided that, if we were to do this, it would be a good idea to take a cruise to Singapore. A major factor was that our passports contained an endorsement for immigration to Australia. Their requirement under the assisted passage scheme was that they should pay virtually all the ticket cost apart from the ten pounds, and we should stay in the country for at least two years. That would be the way, through our labour, that they would have their monies worth from us. Taking a cruise for recreation while we were there wouldn't be wrong. We didn't have a return ticket but the ship wasn't returning for more than a couple of weeks so only having the outward leg ticket was quite a reasonable thing to do, they couldn't stop us from going on holiday. That we didn't have another ticket booked for the return by any other means was a different story, the only one we would have to deal with if confronted. If we were to go, we would have to take the chance. Anyway, on the worst downside, we would end up being taken back to Oz until the end of the two years. It wasn't as if we were going to be sentenced to an additional two years for making our escape, which was something they did some 200+ years before. What we did have to do to hit the immigration regulations in Singapore was to buy a ticket out as they would only give us a visa for a few days. So we took a train ticket into Malaya booked for the next day over onto the mainland via Johor Bahru and on to Kuala Lumpur. As with the cruise from Freemantle to Singapore, we booked the best ticket to start off the trip and this one included a sleeping compartment.

We had been in Oz for five months and saved a little cash but paid more in tax than we had saved. The idea was to try and get that back for the trip home. We applied to do this saying that we were going to have a break from working and travel over to the east coast when we made the application for a refund. Right up until the time we left the authorities said that they would pay us. What we had didn't seem enough for the trip from all accounts of friends that knew friends that had made the trip said it could take many months. A couple of days before the cruise we had still not received the rebate and I called my father to ask if he would wire some cash to us in case we didn't get it. It wasn't so easy then to send money abroad so because we were leaving it was better to send it to a bank in Singapore to collect on the way through. He agreed which was a relief and should get us back amply. As it happened, the cash didn't arrive and we had to go with what we had.

Chapter 5
Settling into the Cruise

We met Gunther on the ship on the first day out of Freemantle.
One of the crew, about our age, saw Chris and me on the deck
having a humorous exchange with a couple of passengers and
asked if we would like a 'welcome on board' beer. Ever the
opportunists Chris and I said sure, why not? We followed him
into the reception area where we thought he was taking us to the
bar. He did a left wheel into the purser's cabin to the side of the
reception. Inside there was the purser and another Asian looking
crew member and another young guy who we guessed from his
accent and name Gunther, was German. The purser an
Australian, full of himself was saying how great it was on the
ship and how we could go to his cabin for drinks. Because of his
rank, he could do us a lot of favours. Although we had a good
cabin, he could find us a better one, even a suite. He knew the
chef who could give us better food than the standard fare and
served specially in our room. We looked at one another and Chris
asked him what we had to do in return. Maybe they wanted us to
bring some girls along. We are thinking only the first day on the
ship and we're getting on great with the crew. "Oh we would
want some favours in return," says the purser.

At that point a different realisation set in, it started to go a
bit weird. "What sort of favours would that be exactly?" I chip
in.

"Well we like you guys and we were hoping you would like
us too," the purser brazenly goes on.

"Well," says Chris, "without putting too fine a point to it, it
looks like you have picked on the wrong people, we would rather
have females to while away the time with." The purser and the
little Asian crew member winced at each other and scowled at us
and at that we both turn to go out of the office. Gunther is still

standing there having not said a word and looking very vulnerable. The crew member also an Australian who had asked us in the first place if we wanted a drink, aggressively stood in between us and the door. The whole thing was about to kick off as we brushed him aside and grabbed Gunther. The Asian guy, the first time of opening his mouth sounded like one of the inhabitants of Boogie Street in a squeaky voice said they should leave us alone as they had made a mistake in singling us out. He did make a gesture about the German guy but we were having none of it. Chris moved the guy from the door and I grabbed Gunther and we opened the door as the purser was still saying how good he could be for us and at least to leave Gunther as he seemed ok with the idea. We told them if they wanted to fuck, they should keep it between them and fuck themselves. The chubby perverted purser then threatened us. "I can make things very difficult for you for this next week, you can't go anywhere away from the ship."

"What the hell are you talking about, we are fare paying passengers." I glared at him.

"You can if you want, if you wish to take it any further we are happy to do so and we will explain to the rest of the crew and captain exactly why." Once or twice we saw him and the other two and we commented on how they were walking funny and perhaps it was not the rolling of the ship but maybe a rolling in the cabin with his boyfriends that caused it. The purser never bothered us directly or Gunther again.

One day we heard both our names called over the address system, "There is a special requirement to enter Singapore where your hair could not touch your collar or ears, would these two passengers please report to the ship's barber for inspection and a cut if we didn't comply with the regulations." Both of us fell about laughing and didn't take any notice. We just thought it was the purser being bitchy. There were other groups of youths that made knowing comments about the purser and his affection for males after hearing the announcement. We said that the only reason we were being hailed was that the purser and his boys already had their way with them being Australian and there being no sheep on the ship. A bit brave as there was nowhere to run to but we got away with it. They commented about a time when we were both cutting our fingernails with clippers we had just

73

bought. "Well having come from the old country, we have learned not to bite them down to the elbow," says Chris.

Come the next morning, we heard the same announcement saying that we must report to the barber or the captain. As we had had the run-in with the purser, we didn't know what to expect. They had been aggressive in the pursers' cabin, maybe the barber was up to the same tricks too or at least in cahoots with the purser and his 'alternate' mob. Maybe the barber would turn out to be a brawny Kung Fu practising his katas round the seats in the shop or Sweeny Todd type character, seriously, what should we expect? We cased the barber's shop to see what he was like watching a couple of people go in and out. He was a 5 foot with little round glasses Chinese, each time he spoke as he finished he bowed his head. He looked ok and not so much a threat but we were still a little concerned. The purser seemed ok as he welcomed us into his office, after how that turned out, anything could happen too. At that, we thought we would go and see the captain and find out if this haircut regulation did apply to non-nationals. The captain saw us, already he had heard of the run-in with the purser and his cronies as the argument at that time had spilt out into the reception. Several passengers and other crew members were able to see and hear what happened as we were making our way out of the office with Gunther. He must have known the purser's persuasion anyway. Although we may not have been the purser's favourite people, he did confirm the haircut instruction. They have been known to send people at customs back onto the ship for a crop before being let loose ashore. Even worse they have the right to refuse entry, never to be allowed in again and that would end up being his problem of what to do with us. As we still had this immigration endorsement stamp problem we thought it better to comply so off we went after saying to the captain if we were accosted by the purser and the barber, we would hold him personally responsible. He laughed and said that there was talk about the fracas in the reception on the first day, he heard that we had dealt with it adequately, and he doubted whether the purser would be taking it any further if we didn't.

We had the haircut with the barber under threat of having to swim the rest of the way to Singapore if he cut it too short. The

Chinaman chuckled. "Yu onry have to come back again if it too wrong still," said the barber.

After doubling up at the barber's accent, Chris says nonsense, just not so short. "Okay for me," says the barber, "I get paid by the twrip anyray." Lo and behold, the next day we have a further announcement. This time it was the purser and with venom in his voice he says, "By specific request of the captain will the two Englishmen, please report to the ship's barber to finish the haircut properly according to the regulations." By this stage, almost everyone on the ship, crew and passengers knew the story. Dutifully we went to see the Chinaman who had a grin from ear to ear. "I towd yu Engrishmen, captain not bery preased a rittle bit."

"Okay," we say to the barber, "we don't want you to be in trouble, cut it as you think."

It was the subject of many conversations after that, all taking the mickey out of the purser. Seriously though, having thought about it afterwards, it was a very difficult situation. If we had not also been singled out at the same time as Gunther, or any other venerable young kids, what was that man able to do and get away with? Imagine a gay pervert, openly taking advantage of the young passengers in that way. The frightening bit of that time was that all the crew knew what was happening; some of the crew were part of it, that's why we had worries about the barber. We had left the captain with him only saying that if we didn't make a fuss out of it, nothing more would be said. He said it in a way that we were man enough to get over it, and we were. We didn't see the guy or his sidekicks with any other young men but maybe there was. Maybe they did find some kid to take advantage of? Worse still, maybe the captain was involved too? It wasn't really good enough to leave it at that.

We had our concerns about the immigration situation and the pending overland trip and had to put it out of our minds. The best we could do was to have a gentle dig with any crew and hoped it would get back to the purser for him to think again. It was something that didn't rest easy with us for some time after. We had dragged Gunther out of danger and spent time with him making sure that he wasn't bothered by them. Still, they brazenly did try again, finding him on his own they would suggest another hookup. He did not say anything and would come looking for us or anyone else that he could find. They did get the message eventually and left him alone.

We were playing table tennis; Chris was pretty good at it from school days. It wasn't so easy to play on a ship rolling with the waves. We were arguing over a point or something, Gunther came and spoke to us. He joined in the game. Feeling confident with us he started to tell us his story. He was going back to Germany as he had upsets with his mother who had gone to Australia with him and her boyfriend (soon to be husband) who Gunther now didn't get along with at all. She had been recently divorced in Germany and was trying to start her life again with her new partner. Gunther was very young for his age of 18 and missed his father hence the decision to leave after a series of rows with his mother's new man. He was old enough to have a constructive view of his relationship with them and from his account, it was an emotional time for them all when he decided to leave. He spoke fondly of his mother and sometimes of the boyfriend but there were some issues he didn't want to deal with.

It was the usual process of the mother terminating the relationship with his father which leaves the child to deal with two other aspects of change. Finishing the relationship with his father also changes the relationship Gunther had with his mother. While a mother and father are together these references become jumbled and at the time of parting the jumbled bits start to be undone as now there is no interdependence of the two, father and son. The son already has adopted some of the traits of the father (which the son through habit thinks are ok) will feel rejection as now the mother doesn't see them as acceptable. The third change is the mother's attention and acceptance of the affections and habits of her new spouse. The son will feel rejected when these are part of the new life because he will not understand why his mother needs them. The mother will also be receiving affections and attention that she hasn't had in the latter part (if ever) of the time with her husband. Her reactions and the interaction between her and her new spouse then appears more alien to the son.

As Gunther spent more time with us, he felt at ease and he took our jibing about the world wars quite well. I saw all the thoughts going on with him that I had been through as an early teenager when my parents decided to part. My mother found someone else, Bernard, went to live with him and after a short while she became pregnant. About six months later, he under massive pressure from his ogre of a first wife with whom he had three children, he decides to go back to her. My mother was distraught but coped very well. She had a few friends that were very good to her and from the time he had gone we never spoke about it.

Earlier going on fifteen, I had a Saturday job, a couple of months had gone by and while at work, Bernhard turned up and asked to talk to me. He started very gently and said it was good of me to speak to him although he thought he didn't deserve it. He trembled as he spoke saying that he had made a terrible mistake and he should never have left my mother and genuinely regretted that he had caused us all trouble. It was obvious that he was speaking the truth, it must have taken a huge amount of strength for him to come to see me and speak of such things as I was going through all these emotions above myself with him and we didn't get along that well at all. Then my mind was racing, he treated me with such respect and was genuinely upset but still kept himself together in what must have been a daunting time in deciding to come to me, and then actually doing it. His appreciation of my feelings and concerns was as humbling for me as it was for him. He asked me if it was ok for him to go to see my mother and ask her if he could move back because he now knew that was what he wanted and needed most of all.

I asked him what had changed his mind and he said that to go was merely the badgering by his first wife about the children and that all the bad parts about her she would check as she now realised that she had been dreadful to him, and the children. Of course in a short while after he returned it was the same. At the same time, he said how much he realised that my mother was so different and good that there was no comparison and he could not imagine living another day with his wife and not another day without my mother. At fifteen this was a lot to compute, particularly as I was dealing with the other stuff that the relationship between I and he was part of. All the anxiety of how it was going to work between us lifted with the strength, honesty and respect that he gave in those few moments but I still somehow managed to remain detached. I told him my view was that it is she who he should be talking to and not me. He quickly replied that my opinion was important to him for it to work. I asked him what he would do if I said no, he said he would have to rethink what he should do as he knew after leaving he didn't have the right to go back. All I could do was to tell him that it wasn't my decision and if it was ok with my mother it had to be ok with me.

My mother didn't know he had spoken to me. He went to see her and within a few days, they were back together. Virtually every word has stayed with me since and it has helped me in discussions about similar situations since and a major step in my development to adulthood from that single day. Enlightening and empowering. We had a kind of respect for each other from then until he, unfortunately, died some years later at a very early age.

--oo--

Gunther had a friend of his family Hans staying in Bangkok and was bound for there but flying from Singapore once he left the ship. All of this Gunther had organised before boarding the ship. He gave us the telephone number of his friends' hotel and said we should meet there if they hadn't left by the time we arrived there. Hans had some experience or knowledge of the best route back to Europe, he was planning to do some of the trip overland and maybe it would be a good idea to travel together or at least exchange notes. We didn't have any notes but it seemed like a good idea. Highly unlikely though that it would happen, thousands of kilometres away in Asia but we would try the number when we arrived there.

At meal times in the restaurant, we would often speak with a Malayan guy. He was about 25 (we still 20 at the time) and always wore a full traditional dress. He said he did it as a protest against the mainly Chinese crew as in his country they were gradually taking over with their large families. Soon the Malays would be in the minority; it was a big political issue there. We said we always thought, when we saw the plight of eastern countries struggling to survive with shortages of food etc., that there wouldn't be enough time in the day to get involved in such finite politics, partly in jest. He said that not all Malays had a problem with having enough food but those that do, blame it and many other things on the Chinese immigrants. He almost came to blows several times with the waiters because they were very disrespectful towards him. We suggested that he toned down the traditional dress a bit but he wouldn't. One day he did end up fighting with one of the waiters and that was the last time we saw him. There was a joke among the other passengers that the kitchen may have made a stir-fry out of him but apparently, he was seen afterwards and was ok of course but after that, he was embarrassed to eat with us.

We docked in the evening time in Singapore. The ship was going on to the islands the following morning, so we spent the final night on the ship without venturing out to the hen house that we had left from our last visit. We had a few drinks with people we had seen each day sailing from Oz and in the morning left on our way to the bank to collect the cash that my father had sent. Chris picked up a packet of local cigarettes to try them. Odd looking things, it was a pack of 10 and when we opened them the tobacco was wrapped in like a thin reed as opposed to a normal cigarette paper. Must be how they make a local brand, thinking no more about it we went for a coffee first and sat and smoked one. By the time we left things were a little bizarre. We hadn't taken the slightest bit of notice of the people around us when suddenly their features became odd. At first, we just thought it was going to be one of those moments where we had a laugh and no more. Not so, for some reason, Chris was worse than I was but we were both hallucinating. The cigarettes laced with drugs were for sale openly on the streets, we had paid 10 Singapore cents for the pack. We took one apart to find out what it was. The reed wrapper was the stalk of a plant of some kind that had been slit along its length, when you do this, put tobacco in the middle and let it go it kind of wraps around itself, so it's ideal for this purpose. Unravelling it exposed some tobacco with small reddish brown bits of what must have been the active ingredients. We were completely daft at that stage and we didn't know if it was illegal or not, paranoid because of the effect and knowing how strict they were over just the haircuts, we threw them away.

Outside the café, we struggled with the map of the city they had given us on the ship. I am usually pretty good with maps but neither of us could make head nor tail out of where we were, never minding where it was we were going so we stopped a taxi and asked him to go to the First National City Bank in whatever street. In the bank, it was worse. It took ages for us to explain to the girl serving us what we wanted and even longer for us to understand what she was telling us. Eventually getting through we made out that the cash had not arrived. We said that was impossible as it had been organised for more than a week, done a few days before we left on the ship, how can it not be here? I was frantic going through the possibilities of what could have gone wrong and what we could do to sort it out as she did say that there was notice of it and more than likely it would be there tomorrow or the next day. It was a lot to compute in our state. We had a visa for twenty-four hours about which they were very strict, and we had already been there 18 of them. Our tickets could not be changed; the usual situation where the price governed their flexibility. If we stayed and it didn't arrive there would be the added expense of the ticket and two days eating expenses and two nights of hotels etc. All this while both of us were completely stoned with the stuff we had smoked in the café bar. Eventually, after pleading with the girl to give us a note to take to the immigration police which she refused, it all failed. We had to decide whether or not to take a flyer with the police. Rather than risk the expense of staying and it not arriving along with the sure difficulties in extending the visas we decided to leave and take a chance on being able to make it with what money we had. After all, it hadn't arrived after ten days; anything could happen from that moment on, it wasn't worth the risk.

Chapter 6
Spam Eggs and Chips

We had so little cash that we then decided to buy some watches and sell them in places as we were travelling. I bought a fur-lined jacket, I didn't have one warm enough, thinking that someone may buy it on the way if it wasn't needed. It was a little desperate but all were very cheap and we were sure would be worth more in Burma or India as these goods were plentiful in Singapore. We also bought watches with the same idea in mind.

The price of the tickets from Singapore to Kuala Lumpur was very cheap because we had booked in advance with a fixed date that was none transferable. We didn't expect much, it was Asia, the accommodation and the meal was all-inclusive. The cabins were clean with fresh linen and the food pretty good too with a choice of meat or fish a starter and a sweet. It was a pleasant rest after the chaos of the city and the disappointment in the bank. It was the start of our journey and it was tiring just being somewhere different and having to make the calculations of what to do next. We were soon to take it all in our stride. The second time in Singapore was different, we were not in a palatial hotel as before, we were leaving on the train but as it turned out, it wasn't too bad at all. This time we were not on our way south to western society, planning on staying and finding jobs and making a social life among English speakers. We were going north, on our way to and through several cultures that we knew little about but knew that they were way different than ours. It was all down to us to get through in that unknown environment which we had no clear idea of how it would be. All we had to go from was what we had seen on the television. We were going into the lands of tribesmen, bandits, cutthroats and thieves; hopefully, we wouldn't meet them all at once and there would be a few good people too. We sat down to the meal on the train knowing that as of this last booked journey, nothing else assured, mind you, that was tomorrow so we decided to enjoy what we had for the time being. We had a map of the world where each country was a different colour and some didn't even have the capital city on them. However, it did give us an idea of direction and the sequence from one country to another. Other than that it was down to whatever facilities and circumstances we could find along the way.

We woke in the sidings in Kuala Lumpur, dressed and went down the platform where I struggled with the backpack while I was looking for my passport. We didn't need them as we had done at Johor Bahru, the border crossing but I was checking. As luck would have it, it was a good job I checked before we left the station as I couldn't find it, I must have left it under the pillow where I had put it for safe keeping. Ug! The station master sent someone to the carriage and we waited in his office until the cleaner came with it in his hand. Phew! He told us how lucky we were, he didn't need to, we knew we were. We walked along for a while in the city but both of us were anxious about the rest of the trip being uncharted and said we had better start walking north to the Thai border. As we walked, we passed beautiful big houses with huge flower-laden gardens which must have been a wealthy part of town. In front of us along the street was a man was opening his car. As we passed, Chris jokingly asked him if he was going to Bangkok by any chance, taking the mickey more than anything. He spoke English and laughed and said how cheeky we were, to our amazement said that he's not going that far but he is going to the northern outskirts of the city if that's any good. It was luck that we would enjoy several times along the journey to the UK and off we went in a new Mercedes. He had no advice except to be very careful as there were many bandits from there to the north.

He asked if we had eaten because he lived down the road from a canteen type place on stilts. He came in to speak to the people there and collect some food and then he left. We sat down at a table and looked at the menu and couldn't make head nor tail out of it. It was about as wild and foreign as can be imagined, in front of us through the window opening with no glass was one straight, flat ribbon of a road that we could see going on for miles, cut through dense jungle. No footpaths, no white lines, no road signs. It looked like we were nowhere and that was exactly where it looked like the road was going. We ate a bowl of rice with a bit of meat that was suddenly placed in front of us. After looking at the menu it was about a penny which didn't matter anyway as when we went to pay on leaving, the guy had paid for us too. We were congratulating ourselves on being able to order the food until we realised the guy had already organised it. It was a nice idea, his thoughtfulness was considerate and uplifting as a complete stranger. While we were in the car we had told him the story of the bank in Singapore and the transfer not being there. He had taken on board that we were short of cash. I also think because he had a far better idea than we as to the magnitude and difficulty of the journey in front of us. He was leaving us in a remote place right at the beginning of the jungle and thought a good meal was in order before we set off into the unknown.

We were beginning to feel depressed as we set off walking, the first time it had happened, up until then, it had been like a holiday with accommodation and transport included. Now all that had changed, we started to think about what would happen if we didn't get a lift as no cars had passed us and we were walking through the night, through the jungle! We had spoken of this in the comfort of the house back in Oz and also mulled it over on the ship to Singapore and thought how exciting and authentic it would be. Now the jungle was our reality, it wasn't so comfortable, it certainly didn't feel excitingly adventurous as we had imagined. It was bleak and our prospects were bleaker by the minute, we felt exposed. We didn't have a comprehension of what was happening, as if all our comfort zone had gone without a trace and there was nothing left that we knew and could rely on. Being able to cope with whatever life threw at us had gone like it was a romantic fantasy, none of that trusted framework to think within.

Just then, when we thought we were at an all-time low and not so confident but putting on a good face to keep up our spirits convincing ourselves that we were capable and up for it, the heavens opened. It rained so hard, in seconds we were ringing wet as if we had just jumped in the sea. I thought we would drown if we took as much as took a breath. We looked at each other and Chris says, "Not much worse than being on the Solway shooting, we'll get through."

He wasn't very convincing and he knew it. I try to shore things up and say, "But here we have the advantage that it's as hot as hell!" with a tremor in my voice, partly because of shouting to be heard over the deafening noise of the rain and partly because I didn't sound convincing either. Both trying to shrug it off, we plodded on.

It was impossible to see more than a few yards and rain hitting the road and the foliage around us was deafening. I shouted to Chris, "Maybe we should go back to the canteen at least it would be dry." Chris said that we were soaked anyway, better that we keep on for a while. It all happened so quickly. Still thinking on our feet, maybe we would come across some shelter for the night of some kind, any kind. By now the rain was so intense it hurt with every drop that landed on us and our shoulders and arms were raw. Maybe there will be a hotel? Some chance of that as after an hour it started to rain heavier, instantly the road was completely awash. Through the torrential rain, we heard a car coming, only the second or third since we started walking. We were out with the thumbs as the car lights appeared we could now work out what it was. In the middle of the jungle in torrential rain as we've never seen before, feeling low and vulnerable in a foreign country showing no mercy was a British racing green Ford Anglia with wide wheels and lowered suspension…….……and it stopped!! We kept pinching ourselves and wondering if this was a jungle version of a mirage and just as it got to us, it would disappear. We touched the car and it felt real, we could tell it was real. The noise of the rain on the car roof and bonnet was deafening, out from behind the wheel came an excited Chinese guy shouting with glee, 'get in, get in quickly', In our minds, we were still trying to compute it all, stunningly he spoke English! He fell over himself to get us two Brits in the car along with our rucksacks etc. The rain was so bad it drenched the seats and interior in the seconds it took to get in. We were so wet that to us it didn't matter but he was a bit upset as we could see that this machine was his pride and joy. At least we weren't now having our heads split with the pressure of rain and within a minute or so we could open our eyes properly as we drove off through the jungle. We were still reeling with amazement, suddenly not in pain from being lashed by the rain, we breathed a sigh of relief which the Chinese guy picked up on.

'Very difficult for many miles to find shelter', he quipped, 'you would surely have been in trouble if I hadn't have found you'. We thanked him profusely and then thanked him again. Another miracle had fallen upon us and it was hard not to wonder how we could be so lucky. To hell with wondering how or why says Chris, as we sped through the jungle. Chris was in the front and me in the back, talking was more like shouting as the rain pelted down on the roof of the car and most words drowned out in the din. We introduced ourselves and found out his name was Charlie. Chris turned around and said, "Charlie? Isn't that what they called the Vietcong?" Charlie didn't hear as he was absorbed in driving straining to see enough road in front of us through the rain, thank goodness. The advantage was that the road was straight for miles but it still took him all his concentration to keep us going safely at a reasonable speed. Maybe says Chris he is a Vietcong and we are haplessly kidnapped and now off to a camp in Cambodia and tortured? Tucking up and still shouting, I say, "More like with the way our luck is running he is taking us off to shag a camp full of wanton native women." That did it, we were in stitches again. We must concentrate to try and help Charlie get us there as he was battling with the wheel in the monsoon, a much better idea. In that moment of sheer relief, we had forgotten the rain was still going on and even though we were now in the car, the problem was still happening. The noise as the sheets of rain hit the car was deafening. Charlie was concentrating on driving which he needed to do for all our sakes but still trying to listen, understand the English and fathom out his two new friends.

He was going to Ipoh a few hundred kilometres north nearer the Thai border. He would take us that far and, perhaps as the jungle became denser from then on it was better we should catch the train which was very cheap all the way up to Bangkok. We were still in awe of our luck, in the dry, a lift and some valuable information, an invite to his sister's wedding party that night and an offer of staying at his house and a lift to the station in the morning. Better still he says, we should stay for a few nights and we could come to the wedding tomorrow and hang around Ipoh. We were beside ourselves, wonderstruck, from the depths of despair again to an incredible comfortable situation. Sometime later the rain had eased off and he drove us to Ipoh and said that he would drop us off at the temple in the mountain while he went to his house to warn his mother and family and ask if it was ok that he was going to bring two foreigners to the house. Maybe the house was where the wanton women are said Chris, as we climb out of the car still pinching ourselves at our luck.

The temple was a very famous tourist attraction; we went inside the caves and through the temple area to the inside which was a volcano type crater. Although we were certainly not spiritual, it was a very spiritual place to be. The air was very still and deadly quiet apart from faint intermittent, hollow cracking noises. The crater was about a hundred and fifty meters in diameter at its base with virtually vertical sides at least a hundred meters high. Flowers, trees and shrubs grew from cracks in the rock, it was very old, established over centuries. Macaque monkeys roamed the temple site and on the crater walls. At the base, there were two large ponds. As we walked over to them, it became apparent what the cracking noise was. The ponds were full of turtles and the cracking noise was them banging into one another and the shells touching, the sound was like the hollow tubes the priests knock to make that eerie religious sound that you hear in connection with temples but this sound was natural. There was an uncanny peace about the place that was difficult to explain. You could physically feel calmness filtering into you, it had such a presence and serene effect on your body and mind. Just what it's supposed to do I guess.

It was certainly a place of thankful worship to us now as only a few hours before we were at our wit's end wondering if we would ever find a dry, warm place to sleep without being battered by the rain and thinking if we didn't die from that, maybe the bandits would get us. Just then our friend Charlie returned saying that they were cooking food for us and we should go there now. He was so open and pleased to have found us it was as if we were pulled along in a whirlwind of kindness, even the family wanted to meet us. In the temple, I said to Chris that I was thinking to stay and convert to Buddhism, with all this luck maybe it was an omen directing us to our vocation. I think he said something like, "Are you out of your fucking mind?"

I said, "Yes, I think so."

He said something along the lines of, "So am I so don't tempt me, I've been feeling a bit blessed myself, do they serve

Boddingtons?" We laughed at the very idea of even thinking of even the word Boddingtons in such a place as three or four orange clothed priests going 'um' walked past us. "They could be the brewers," says Chris, so both of us chuckled again. They saw we were amused at something they smiled in a quiet quizzical way. I said I wondered if they spoke English, we could explain what it was that we were amused at, I was quite willing to try, we were usually game for anything and this would be a challenge. Chris backed off which was unusual for him thinking quite innocently, it was too complicated and perhaps we were crediting them with more understanding of foreigners and their ways. They may think we were taking the mickey out of them. Maybe we were. We carried on our way through the rock tunnels through the mountain crater sides to the exit. It was extremely weird, we were in such a remote and to us, an alien place and yet so at ease. An almost unimaginable contrast from a few short hours ago of being anxious and depressed hammered by the rain before the arrival of Charlie and a lift that took us out of that very difficult set of circumstances. Was that part of a spiritual experience or just plain luck? Whatever.

Charlie had parked at the front of the temple and we jumped into the car. It seemed odd that such a highly spiritual place was so accessible that you could park your car at the entrance. We seemed to think it should be more isolated, at the end of a long walk or something that created an end of where you came from. No matter, maybe this was purposeful to bring this uncommercial world of ours closer to their way of life. In minutes we were sitting around the kitchen table of the house, a two/three bedroomed semi somewhere in the outer part of Ipoh. I remember thinking that we could have been in a suburb of an English town, it seemed so familiar. Suddenly, in front of us landed a plate of spam, eggs and chips. Chris and I stared at each other in disbelief, he was pinching himself and chuckling. If someone had told us some 6 or 7 hours earlier what we would be doing now, we would have asked what brand of those funny cigarettes they had been smoking. It was all just too fantastic to be true and we couldn't help wondering if in relating the experience to others, they would think we were making it up. It would be understandable because it was happening to us there and then, we were even verging on not believing it too! Since leaving the train we had been through so many emotions and experienced so many unpredictable events in wildly different environments and circumstances. We had only just started out, what was the rest of it going to hold for us. Just let's hope the luck would hold, surely it couldn't.

The guests arrived that evening for a party and barbecue, all lovely people just as excited as was our friend Charlie to meet us. We talked to everybody; all wanted to know what we were doing there and where we were going. The whole family was there along with some from the groom's side. We were very conscious that we were starting to be the centre of attraction and, as they were there for a much bigger celebration than the appearance of two foreigners, we felt uncomfortable soaking up the attention, so we told Charlie it was better we left. Charlie, of course, was very quick to assure us that no one thought that way and we were more than welcome. It was as much of a spectacle to them as it was a miracle to us that we were there under these circumstances. The whole place was full of nervous chatter. Eventually, after another couple of hours, we were horsed and a little bewildered through talking to so many different people, someone called the train station and found that there was a train leaving around 3.30am going all the way north to the border and then on to Bangkok. We had got to know many people and they wanted us to stay for the wedding and beyond but the next train to go through with only one change wasn't for another three days. It was an opportunity we would like to grasp as it would take us north for about 1300 kilometres, on the train in dry conditions, a little something we had just learned to take into serious consideration and appreciate from our first day of hitchhiking. We drank beer and wine and danced all evening with some very interesting Chinese girls and were very tempted again to stay for the wedding but we stuck with the plan.

They took us to the station for about 2.30am and made sure that we were on the right train as by now we had much to drink and we collapsed until it was light. The scenery was open fields with crops and then plunged back into thick forestation. We had travelled relatively slowly for about 250 km stopping and starting, now we were somewhere near the Thai border. It was such a relief that we were sitting in the dry and comfort of the carriage, if we had been going at a snail's pace it would not have mattered. Progress dry and without pain was fine, the people around us friendly.

It happened very quickly as we saw Malaysia disappear into the distance and rode into Thailand. We had stepped down off the train, a cursory glance at the passports by immigration, handed over a completed rudimentary visa form which they gave us at the station in Ipoh, and were directed after some noisy shunting and shouting onto another train. It was impossible to take the wrong train as there was only one platform, not only was there only one platform but there was only one rail track. We were asleep so didn't know what had happened for much of the trip on the Malay side or when the other tracks had disappeared. Ipoh was quite a big station with several platforms and lines but now there was only one of everything. Every so often we would pull into a siding track and another train would pass us going the other way. Very primitive through dense jungle and mountain passes, we sat in one siding for a day and a half waiting for the oncoming train. There was no explanation we just sat among all the local families; no one seemed to bother about the delay, children were playing in the aisles and on the banking next to the train. We still remembered the rain and pain as a thing of the past and grateful for the relaxation.

People came from the surrounding villages with food for the passengers, mostly spicy rice cooked with vegetables and lemon grass wrapped in banana leaves and tied with thin strips of what seemed to be green bamboo type fibres. Sometimes they brought meat with the rice along with as much fruit as you could eat. After a while, we got the hang of ignoring the sellers until their prices were the same as the locals paid until the cost was not even a consideration. The meat packages were five times more than the vegetable packs but still pennies in the scheme of things. Folks on the train were happy with their lives; it was as if the locals selling the food were close friends of the passengers. It was almost impossible as they were from hundreds of kilometres away and they were all simple village people and not seasoned international business travellers. We stopped at countless stations where some of the passengers would leave and others replace them, some stayed for the duration. Few of the original passengers were still with us in Bangkok so clearly, they were travelling between villages over long distances for whatever reason. By far the majority of the passengers were women and children and I don't remember seeing anyone in western clothing. It was a pleasure to be amongst them, although said little they made us welcome. The women encouraged the children to bring us food and water all for the sake of being polite without adding to the cost and some they brought from their food prepared at their homes, obviously used to the long journey that they shared with us without needing money. You could not wish to see and experience better ethnic Thai life, as it must be for the majority of people outside of the cities.

On a more sober note, compared to the western world, the toilets left a lot to be desired, after only a short distance the tap water for washing ran out to be infrequently replenished. Not being able to use them unless the train was moving, made the day and a half in the sidings a little uncomfortable. The carriages were open and seats were wooden bench types all good quality and not worn or shabby, mostly two and two facing each other with a centre aisle separating one side from the other. No upholstery or the like so we used towels as cushions rather than spend such a long period sitting on a wooden bench. The women kept the carriage clean and tidy from rubbish that the children inevitably produced. All in all, it was a relaxing trip and very much existing alongside the native people who were nothing but good to us. The Thai people had a peace with them that we carried for some time. As we left the train we had to consciously bring ourselves out of a trancelike state we were in, then tune into the now very different metropolitan surroundings. It is difficult to describe just how captivating the last what seemed to be weeks but only four days had been. They welcomed us into local Thai villager's way of life without scepticism or fear and it all seemed very natural. It was a pleasure being with them.

It was the beginning of day five as we pulled into Bangkok station that morning. We were filthy and must have smelt terrible with only bottled water to wash with most of the time. The hubbub of the city was a rude awakening to the laid back train journey among very welcoming countryside village people. In the station we were bombarded with 'make a few baht youngsters', all with the best deal in town for accommodation and money changing. After the train journey, we felt at ease and confident that we and didn't have to think so much about being abducted by bandits or the like. We took a chance on one hotel offer and after a short ride in a rickshaw thing, we were opening the door of a 'palace for 50 pence' per night for the two of us including a scant breakfast. We took long showers to be rid of the four days of ingrained dust and sweat and started to feel human again, ate some local food organised by the receptionist in the hotel and then phoned to see if we could find Gunther.

To our surprise, he was still there with his friend Hans and arranged to meet the next day. I say surprised because that's just what we were. Now a week into our overland trip so much had happened. We changed; we were different people every day. When we thought back to our attitude while on the outward leg from the UK and landed in Singapore, we thought we were seasoned travellers back then. By the time we were organising to leave Australia, we had thought that we knew just about everything. The fact was we had seen and knew next to nothing and had no in-depth experience of life in a foreign country and the people there. Each day from stepping on to the train in Singapore brought another whole encyclopaedia of new experiences and knowledge that we had no idea about the very day before! What we were starting to realise and believe was that the crux of it all was the people, it was them and their attitude towards us that made it, and they were the trigger to this wealth of humanism in life we were experiencing. The short lift out of Kuala Lumpur and the food the guy bought for us, the lifesaving lift from Charlie the Chinese, the spam, eggs and chips and his family at the wedding party, the train journey with Thai families. The country was happening around us with sights unique to where we were, but it was the people themselves that were responsible for us taking the best out of the experience. They were not tour operators or hospitality employees helping and encouraging us because it was their job. They did it because that is what they were, good-hearted thoughtful people wanting us to be comfortable in their environment and they were happy to share that with us. They wanted us to part having had a pleasurable experience for good memories. There is always the risk of being lulled into a false sense of security when something weird happens out of the blue. We tried to keep this in mind.

We were now back in the contrasting commercial world with city life around us, the recent experiences strengthened us but things were different now we were in the metropolis. There was a small lounge in the hotel and during the evening a few people, some other travellers and some expat semi-locals, would meet and talk. Someone agreed to go and find some beers and pizza. At one point an American turned up, he was the one selling international press cards and student union cards. He explained that there were huge discounts to be had in every country all the way back to England if that's where we were going. It didn't make a lot of sense to us at first. Official cards, exactly as they appeared in London or Berlin or New York. How on earth could that be done for anyone to believe they were real to save the sorts of cash they were known to do? We would save a fortune on bus, rail and plane tickets alone, we made another call when he had left to check it out with Gunther's' friend and he said it was true and they were well worth having. The American guy had agreed to come back in the morning and Gunther and Hans would come over and buy some too. Still not sure how it was possible, we went to the room and slept like logs quite confident that we had laid down at least a small plan so as not to be beaten to death by that horrendous rain again. In the morning we were all there in the lounge wide-eyed.

Sure enough, the American opened up a huge case that contained a selection of student union cards from universities and press cards from newspapers in every major country all over the world, all we needed were the pictures which we arranged earlier that morning before he came and that was that. Stunning, by the time he had finished the four cards for Chris and me, he had us believing that we had been to Lancaster University. Right now we were on a fact-finding mission about soldiers on rest and repose from Vietnam in Asian countries for the Daily Telegraph in London or something similar. A polished and fundamentally enlightening service, now it would be an absolute piece of cake presenting them to travel agents etc., to have the discounts. Magic! No one ever questioned their validity.

Picture cropped, stuck in position, signed and laminated on the spot, all for $5 each. By the time he had finished we willingly paid the skilful supplier $10 each. They saved us a lot of money on tickets from then on. On the flight from Bangkok, we saved $50, if we hadn't, we couldn't have afforded them. They governed our progress majorly as these and other flights would have been prohibitive without the discounts they provided.

That morning also we finally met Hans at the illicit card counterfeiting session, they also dipped their boots. It became obvious why Gunther teamed up with him. Hans was older than Gunther, about thirty I would say. Far more worldly than Gunther which was pretty much what we expected. He needed him as the father figure he missed from home in the same way as he had taken to us from that first moment when we dragged him out of the purser's office on the cruise from Australia. More interestingly to us, Hans had been to some of the places we were to travel through and knew people that had made the trip across Asia. He had been in Bangkok around travellers meeting points for some time. He was a valuable source of information. So indeed was the American with the cards. He was meeting people every day while selling his cards in hotels in Bangkok who were on the same trek going back to Europe but also coming from Europe. These people would tell him stories from the places visited and do's and don'ts which came in handy.

It would appear that generally the route now was Burma, India, Pakistan, Afghanistan, Iran and Turkey. Altogether a massive education and helped to dispel some of those very isolated feelings of not knowing what the hell to do next. There was lots of information and there were many things to remember. You could not cross the land border from Thailand to Burma or the one on the other side of Burma to India, which meant a flight unless you wanted to take a chance, go to the border and try to bribe an official to cross. Likewise, since the problems in the temple in Amritsar, there has always been trouble with the land border from there to Lahore in Pakistan; sometimes it was open, sometimes not. All of this needed thought and as much information as we could gather from other travellers coming the other way. We were now experienced travellers. It was the first time Chris digested the idea that others sense of direction and experience might have an advantage over his uncalculated wet finger in the air and next folly was the right thing to do. He knew already but confirmation from the experienced people did have its effect. It did with both of us; suddenly there were other people with which we could talk over things we would do from now were not just guesswork.

So, for the first time, we now had formulated a skeleton route to travel by country and a few aiming points within them, even so, we still had a fair task ahead of us, the information was invaluable. There were still big holes in the plan and the details of how we would cross each country to the next worked out as we went. It was both daunting and exciting but as we were making ground, we learned every day from the experiences. We had also started to clock up useful information for us to impart in return having done the southern part of Thailand and Malaya. Most importantly we had some luck and some incredible luck which appeared to be the best and most desirable ingredient needed. Bring it on!

Chapter 7
Leaving Bangkok

Gunther and Hans went off to meet friends of Hans who lived in Bangkok. They had plans to do other things but after a few days they would set off on the same route we were advised to take. First, we had to book the flight tickets so we thought we would take the opportunity to go to one of the floating markets in the sprawling city. It was fascinating. Busy, bustling and noisy, everyone seemed to be talking at the same time. Here you could buy whatever you wanted. From fast food to vegetables, meat and fish, canned and dried food of every sort you wanted along with grotesque things hanging from the sun shades or in jars you can never imagine wanting. Ironmongery and household goods, trainers and football shirts all at ultra-low prices stacked precariously on their small paper thin, also dangerously low to the water boats. How they all stayed afloat was a miracle. Especially when some impatient and careless trader decided he would make his way through them at speed creating a wash that spilt over the sides of semi-moored sellers desperately hanging on with one hand while passing over their wares with the other and trying to collect the cash with one hand less than was needed. They deserved every penny they gathered.

Sightseeing, although we wanted to relax and enjoy the enormously unusual and varied sights, was marred because we still had not solved the problem of being short of cash for the journey. We had changed the cash for travellers' cheques but we only had around 100 GBP each having paid for the voyage from Freemantle which was a bit of an extravagance because we had taken one of the more expensive cabins. The major blow was not collecting the cash my father was to send to us. In Singapore we had bought some warm clothes in anticipation of the colder climates we would have to pass through and bought some cheapish watches which they assured us we could sell in India for a healthy profit.

At this point, we knew we had to do whatever it takes to survive on the journey having not collected the cash my father had organised in Singapore. A ruse with the traveller's cheques was another idea from Hans as he knew we didn't have so much to last for the whole trip without making some extra cash along the way. We could say that we had lost them and have them replaced. The old ones, which we hadn't lost, would be in demand here and in India too and we could find a buyer among the money changers of which there would be scores. We duly reported them missing at the nearest police station. Inadvertently we'd left them in a rickshaw on the way back from the market and as there were thousands of them and they all looked the same as did the drivers. After a few questions, we received the official report, stamped and ready for a visit to the issuer's office and unbelievably they replaced them. There were many money changers interested in buying in Bangkok too but we thought better not to sell them there. Better to hang on to them until India.

After using the student union cards for the flight tickets to Rangoon and then on to Calcutta we had about 75 GBP each left but things were looking good and we were making real progress and feeling pleased with ourselves. Having jumped through hoops with the plan for the cheques and fixed a considerable chunk of the next part of the trip, we decided to have a meal in one of the cafes along the river. Fish and seafood was the order of the day after our financial coup of the cheques and an unbelievable 50% off the flights! We found an authentic café and were still tucked up with laughter after relating a story to a couple of local girls in the travel agency. We told them about being stoned while we were in Singapore and had them crying with laughter as we were explaining who we were and what we wanted from the bank. I suspect that if we hadn't have been 'out of it' at the time, we might have come up with an idea of how to stay and wait for the cash to arrive. It would have been sensible given that without it we were severely short of money for the journey (as we didn't have a clue about how and what we would have to deal with and what would be the cost) but we just weren't sensible after smoking the dope. In our defence, we had discounted the idea of extending our stay in Singapore remembering the hoo-ha of the haircuts on the ship before entry and how manic they were about obeying the law. We didn't think they would have allowed the extension so didn't even consider it; maybe foolishly we just put it out of our minds.

The seafood etc., the beers and the relaxation were very welcome. The flight was for not the next day but the following morning after. Although an expense for staying another day we felt pretty good about ourselves for the progress made to date and the organising of the next stage of the trip. In our minds, we had accepted a manageable degree of being 'strung out' as normal. Put another way, it was normal to be a little 'strung out' as what we were doing now was part of the nature of the trip, it was just a case of being more vigilant on a minute to minute basis. Sounds better than being 'strung out' we thought, Up to then we had not even thought of relaxing. We shouldn't have been so hasty as little did we know how different the next 36 hours would develop in an unimagined way and take all our strength to make sure that we managed to make the flight.

We got back to the hotel with a few beers and, after a call to the Germans, Gunther and Hans thinking they could come to the hotel for the evening; they turned down our invite, so we settled in for the evening of beers on the balcony. It was hot and humid balmy evening. Lizards ran along the ceiling and walls and the by now standard background Asian conversational cackle was ever present around us in the hotel grounds adjoining properties and from neighbouring balconies. We were on the first floor and had a view by way of outside lighting over the brightly coloured flowers in the garden grounds and beyond the rambling city lights as far as could be seen in the distance. The warm breeze was comforting and a perfect time to sit while digesting our meal from earlier in the evening with a few beers we had picked up.

There was a knock at the door. Instantly both of us thought of the warning Hans gave us about locals trying to rob foreigners in hotels. Chris called out asking who it was and a high pitched female voice replied, 'room service'. It was confusing as we hadn't asked for anything. Naively we both thought that maybe the two Germans had changed their minds and decided to visit and had sent the girl from reception to tell us they were here. I stood back while he opened the door and there in the corridor were two young girls giggling. With a smile on his face, 'What do you want?' says Chris. One girl still giggling stood back while the other moved towards him and put her hand on his crotch and says, "You wan' fucky Jonny, anyfin' you wan', wha' you wan' Jonny?" It certainly was room service, personal and very friendly. We both look at each other severely tempted. Chris asked if we could afford it but even for the initially $10 requested then down to $5 (for whatever basic service) we were still concerned about the cash and reluctantly declined. They saw we were considering the expense and hung around outside the door for some time in case we changed our minds. We sat back down on the balcony with the beers and the niggling doubt of the wisdom of our decision and wondered if we had driven them harder it would have been less. Eventually, it went out of our minds thinking that it was wiser, safer and cheaper at this time (even the prostitutes will fleece you) to keep things clean. We relaxed back into taking in the view and enjoying the close, warm evening air feeling smug in our abstinence.

During the night we each paid calls to the bathroom and didn't give it another thought until woke in the morning, very ill with bad stomachs. It must have been something in the seafood from the afternoon before mustn't have been good. It could have been the salad washed in the local water but whatever, it was bad, very bad. After all, we couldn't have caught something from the tarts! We spent the whole day in bed virtually except trips back and forth to the toilet and ate nothing. Waking the following morning, the morning of the flight to Rangoon, we were still in trouble. I was bad but Chris was delirious and could hardly speak, scary, I had never seen him like that before. We managed to pack our kit, went down to the reception and out on to the street. Bundled everything into a rickshaw and went off to the airport. As we went through the entrance doors, Chris dashed the toilets and I went to check us in. After a while I thought by now he should have been back but no sign. Another five minutes of waiting and I went off to look for him.

No sign or response to a call inside the toilet, there was one of the cubicles closed. I walked over to the door and pushed gently, it was locked, I called again but again no response. By this time I was worried, he was very ill and had been in a state since getting out of bed, and could have been anywhere in his delirium. We didn't have very long before we had to go through to the departure lounge. I took a chance and jumped up at the closed cubicle door but didn't rise high enough, apart from the commotion just jumping to get high enough to see in, I would have to pull myself up using the top of the door. That would be a total commitment if it wasn't him in there. It would be horrifying enough and virtually impossible to get over with some paranoid Thai abluting in peace, but an old person could have a heart attack or something similar at a foreign stranger appearing to break into his cubicle. I started to imagine how I would explain it all to the Thai airport police. Tempest Fugit as they say and I had to make the decision and taking a deep breath I grabbed the top of the door and briefly popped up to see inside. Phew! Thank goodness it was him in there was my first thought relieved I had not got to spend time at the police station explaining what it was that I was trying to do. There he was, completely passed out on the pan and that's why he hadn't responded. He was so ill he had lost consciousness. It was so out of character. As a rule, he was as sharp, bright as a button, quickest wit of anyone, always cracking jokes and seeing a humorous, crazy side in most situations. For him to completely tune out, he must have been seriously badly. I had to stop myself thinking it could even be fatal. He just slumped, part sitting on the seat, ashen and listless not even hearing me. As I started to climb over the door, I was seriously worried about his health, having got beyond the uncomfortable thought of disturbing a strange Thai on the toilet, I still wondered how I would explain what I was doing to any strangers that came in. I was making one hell of a noise squeezing in between the top of the door and the ceiling. With most of my weight now over the door on the cubicle side and with no footing to climb down slowly, I lost my concentration worrying about the legal implications of being discovered, overbalanced and fell forward head first virtually onto his lap into a heap on the floor in the small space left in the cubical. I remember in a flash thinking of one day in the UK an older guy working outside on a first-floor bay window roof with no ladder or safety gear while I was walking along a street in Poulton. I called to him and said, 'you be careful up there, it's a long way to fall'. Quick as a flash he said, 'the falling is ok, it's the deceleration at the bottom that's a problem'. Half laughing and half frantic, and suffering from the similar stomach trouble and now a few bruises, I picked myself up, brought him around a bit and unlocked the door. Thank the lord nobody disturbed us at that point, moaning I lifted him up from the pan with his pants around his ankles as I am saying, "Come on Chris shape up before someone sees us!" He came to a little and realised what was happening and realising the farcical situation started to laugh. At that stage, which wasn't good because it started us both off, I thought he might have lost control running the risk of him crapping on the floor. Only we could have got into such a state. At least with the humour, he was now a little more responsive and although he still didn't know where he was, he was far more alert.

He was still in a daze, not making much sense and he didn't care. After explaining that we couldn't afford to lose the tickets being discounted concessions, cheap and not changeable. Eventually, he cleaned himself up dressed and we staggered out of the toilet and through the airport. Somehow we managed to get to the departure lounge where I had some help with him from the airline staff after a patchy explanation of the predicament. Within a few minutes they opened the gate and we followed the other passengers and stepped on the bus to the plane.

Both of us stood there staring as we got off the bus. The plane was small, I mean tiny. It was so small one fat guy at the top of the boarding stairway seemed stuck in the door opening with his case. They managed to get him in and then it was our turn. No sooner had we got inside having to walk sideways along the narrow aisle, we were through a simple fabric curtain and with the pilot in the cockpit. The pilot looked shocked and asked what we were doing in there. That we ended up there might sound weird but remember both of us were ill and not totally together, it was as much of a shock for us to be in the cockpit as it was for the pilot. We had been used to much bigger planes and just continued along the aisle looking for two seats together. Involuntary and defensively I said I was looking for a seat for my friend who was ill. He said, "Well, your seats are back there."

I said, "I know but the plane is so small, I thought there were more seats. I was just looking for somewhere quiet for him." The stewardess came along and sat us both down, Chris spent the next while looking longingly at the toilet door. Thankfully it was the same crew from the departure lounge and they had the basic story to reference. Before we had even taxied to the runway Chris was trying to make his way to the toilet, the girl calmed him and he held himself until the overhead lights went out. After that he was straight in and there he stayed for a good part of the flight into Burma. He came out in better humour having sat quietly on his own for some time while gathering his thoughts.

The whole episode was hilarious and at the same time embarrassing. The two stewardesses were just as embarrassed. Both stunning looking, dressed in their native style uniforms of bright white, lace-cuffed and collared blouses, turquoise jackets and skirts with matching turquoise pillbox hat to compliment the outfit, delicately placed on their heads a little off centre and slanting. She was concerned about us being ill but she was captivating, something to appreciate even without her empathy for our circumstances. I mused recalling the episode at the airport and thinking how difficult, if it had gone wrong, it would be to explain yet, in a flash, the stewardess caught my glimpse and understood precisely what was happening. It would not be easy and instantly explained and understood with a hairy assed airport policeman…or policewoman.

Through the window, the bit of a view I had was also captivating. Just about all the different scenes, you could imagine in the exotic Far East. Some villages with odd buildings around them, rolling lush green hills and regimented sectioned flat areas which I assumed were rice fields or similar. There were mountains and passes, jungle areas that went on for miles. Even high in the sky, I had a genuine feel for what it was like down on the ground. It brought to mind the sort of scenes you would see in a Vietnam War movie, albeit that it was Thailand and Burma, lush and calm without wind and a kind of deadly quiet brought about in countryside heavy and warm humidity, in between fighting scenes that is. So now feeling a little mellower and taking stock of how differently the last thirty-six hours had been compared to the relaxed day and a half we expected after booking the flight tickets at the travel agents and then spoiling ourselves with a nice meal. All in life's tapestry as Chris regularly said.

Finally, we were on the approach to Yangon airport and after a shaky start at getting out of the seats when we had landed, we were out of the airport on the bus, along with the stewardesses from the flight on the way to the hotel. Our connecting flight to Calcutta was in the morning of the following day. The people we saw on the way were in traditional Burmese dress.

We bartered for what seemed like hours with the hotel desk clerk. We had not budgeted or even known of this overnight expense from the travel agent in Bangkok and got the cheapest rooms available.......close to the toilet of course after the full explanation, both of us still having issues with after effects of the seafood meal. The rooms were just partitions, over a large floor area with corridors in between blocks, that didn't go all the way up to the ceiling with a curtain as a door. It was a little disconcerting not being secure, but it was clean and organised. The night passed with a few visits to the toilet but the pains had subsided and it was obvious that the worst had passed.

We did manage some basic breakfast in the morning and felt a million per cent better than the previous day and jumped on the bus to go back to the airport. Knowing that the stomach recovery had set in gave us a charge we needed. The hotel was literally on the road running alongside the Irrawaddy. The river was incredibly wide and the flow was ferocious to be in the middle of a city. The water deeply coloured with mud, filthy and choppy with chaotic waves like an angry sea. Flimsy boats with long shaft outboard motors were making their way across and back, they must have been some form of taxi or similar. The flow was such that they would have to face upstream at the severe angle of 45 degrees or more to end where they wanted to be and not washed to a point further downstream. Drivers/captains getting it a fleeting second wrong would have created a disaster at any time as they piloted them across to the safety of the other side. It was also overcast which took a lot of the colour from the surroundings and made it seem even more menacing. You think about these exotic places and have a picture of what it would be like but this unromantic and frightful picture you would never have imagined. Life was so tricky, even as a local water taxi driver (of local sorts) you took your life in your hands not just on the odd occasion, these severe environmental circumstances were present all day, every day and dealt with as a matter of course. We fuss over a cycle or bus lane being an inconvenience in our everyday life!

As we waited outside the hotel one of the little apparitions from the inbound flight crew stood on the pavement in her clean, pristine uniform regalia. Anyone that has spent time in the Far East and been involved with the people, particularly as a hot-blooded western male, cannot with all sincerity say that they have never been captivated by at least one of the eastern women if only for a second. Eastern girls emit a girlish calmness without even knowing that you are looking or paying attention. It is not necessarily sexual, although not far short; it's friendly and good. Captivating but nothing like the invigorating and intense, homely and humour aware as the red-haired British girl on the plane on the way out, only a few months back which now seemed many years ago.

This young Burmese stewardess was very pretty and looked coy as we drooled at the bus window. She smiled as she saw us looking at her then lifted her head in the air and cleared her throat before she turned to the side thank goodness for what followed, and spat it out in the gutter. Well, you could have knocked us both over with a feather. Such a delightful young thing, butter wouldn't have melted in her mouth and hardly looked old enough to be out of school. Well, another reality just set in. We were on the banks of the Irrawaddy and not in the tea rooms in the Trough of Bowland by the river Lune or Wyre.

-oo-

The plane from Rangoon was much the same as the the one from the day before, two engines with propellers but substantially bigger and less noisy. Altogether less worrying than the last one and by this time, both in a different frame of mind with much more calm stomachs and rested after the night's sleep. Chris was nearer his old self. Albeit that we flew, which was not how we envisaged travelling preferring to take in the sights and local people and events, we had a sense of achievement by putting miles behind us. We didn't expect to have large chunks of travelling in the air, leaving a partial thought in mind of having missed out on what was happening on the ground covered. Not that we hadn't seen or experienced anything. Much had happened and we had a more knowing sense and awareness of what was happening and where we were for the diverse places and situations we had passed through an experienced. It was kind of a sense of growing up. On the plane on the way out from the UK we flew the whole time over countries from the Middle East to the Far East and I can remember thinking how much more enlightening and enjoyable it would be to be in those places. From a plane your perspective is so much removed from the actual life there so much so in fact, it is a distraction from what really is. However, it's a whole lot quicker and certainly has its advantages to get from one place to another in a short period.

Being involved with boats from being kids established the principle that life is as much about getting there as being there and the journey is as much of the experience as your experience of the destination. The journey is also a personal achievement and particularly where you have circumstances to deal with such as inclement weather, terrain, difficult people and unfamiliar cultures, systems and protocol to take into account. If you were flying the plane and not just being a passenger, now that would be different and would be an achievement. If the course you are following is not new and you have done it before you still have to deal with whatever changes to the circumstances of the day. Part of the enjoyment is perfecting the journey by way of distance or fuel saving, getting the best out of the facility you are using etc. We had set off from the UK with the expectation of the journey back will be at least as important as the being in Australia if not more so. When travelling the scenery changes all the time, it leaves less room for you to tire of the immediate environment. You meet with different people and have to deal with circumstances and situations that more than likely are unfamiliar. Fundamentally we could make a situation out of nothing, as was the case of the plane journey out. Continually changing circumstances are more demanding and require more mental effort and agility, far more absorbing. Travel does broaden the mind but it does far more than that in that the mental activity expands the ability to think better or clearer allowing you to deal better with whatever circumstances befall, continually trying to make the most and best of wherever you are with and whatever you become involved.

Our experiences had been rich and satisfying and with a healthy carefree attitude to whatever we would encounter or confront next. Granted we had the continual advantage that we didn't have much of a clue as to what the following experience was going to be. If we had, it might have depressed or discouraged us, though not much I suspect. By that time we were mentally flying on the adrenalin of having survived to that point and proud of the achievement. Our only main concern was the cash situation but even that was a challenge. Hopefully, we were going to deal with this in part and for the time being on arrival in India with the plan of selling the watches and the cheques but even then, having never done such a thing before, we had no idea how that would turn out. At least we were making a few more miles and creating a bit more time before we had to worry. With a little anticipation, we landed in Calcutta, Dum Dum airport, what a name! It is a district around 10 km from the city also gives its name to the dum dum bullet made in a factory in the district. We travelled again to the city by airline bus to find one of the most shocking places I had certainly ever seen or heard of.

Chapter 8
Life's Cheap

It was a complete mish-mash. People are walking, running, gesticulating in argument milling around or appearing to be in a hurry, a race with each other and seemed to be using any method they could to be first. What at or where to, nobody looked like they knew. If they had an overall purpose that wasn't just this frantic action displayed, it was lost a long time ago and what they were doing now was just a manic habitual usage of energy. Something they had to do to fill the time of day. With all manner of dress types, suits and native clothes some clean and tidy others scruffy and filthy. Disabled and mutilated half-clothed children were sat on the pavements and in the gutter among filth and litter. Street after street of street sellers of just about every item you could think of alive or dead. Road junctions where four or five or more roads converge with one traffic policeman in the middle not having the slightest idea of who should go first and road users pull rickshaws, bicycles and motorbikes, cars and three-wheeled auto-rickshaws, buses and trucks alike doing their own thing. Everywhere you looked it was chaos and several chaoses's going on at the same time. Triple and quadruple chaos in each of three or four places. Chaos as far as you could see and wherever you went. There was no escape from sheer chaos. We couldn't take it all in, people and families with babies living on the street, people washing at a standpipe. So much was happening when we arrived at the bus terminus and we felt completely alienated. We took one look at each other and decided that, as our next point to aim at was Delhi, it was perhaps a good idea to find out how to head there as soon as it was earthly possible, the first impression of India was that it was best behind us. Our guess was the train, after a few enquiries the train station was miles away. We stood at the bus terminus for a while trying to digest the activity but the only way you could describe it was deprived, disgusting and dangerous chaos. Before long we made a 'friend'. A guy latched on to us and said that for a small fee which we would agree, he would make sure we got to where we wanted to go. As we were discussing the merits, there was a young boy of about eight years old hanging around behind us and tugging at our clothes eagerly trying to take the business from the older guy. Both of us were overwhelmed with the sheer degree of poverty displayed in the whole place. It wasn't just a few poor people among others that had their stuff together, everyone was poor and destitute. It took some believing and was upsetting; this was the hardest place to deal with and the very reason to get the hell away from a frightful Calcutta.

We decided to employ the young boy after we grasped his story of being the only wage earner in the family of I forget how many. The older guy kept shouting at and hitting the lad and telling him to go away. Both of us grabbed the guy to stop him, which was all a bit worrying as we were the foreigners and anything could have been believed to be happening. As they say, never argue with an idiot because onlookers from a distance find it hard to distinguish the difference. Two of us fighting off the Indian…in India could have been construed wrongly and badly for us. It was hard to grasp how violent and desperate the guy was. We took the boy to one side and as he had some English told him we needed to go to the train station. As we set off the older guy was still screaming and still trying to get at the boy as he followed us for several blocks. Eventually, he gave up and, as we were not making so much headway through the crowds on the pavement, the boy convinced us to take a pull rickshaw after he had the driver to agree to take the bit of Burmese and Thai currency we had in payment for the trip. We stepped into the rickshaw and the boy dutifully ran alongside.

The chaos continued along with the depravity in all of the streets of Calcutta. I couldn't help thinking of the term 'Black Hole of Calcutta' wasn't such a bad description, although it wasn't black, just a dirty, littered grey-brown colour, the 'hell hole of Calcutta' was a more apt term for the place. It took a lot to unnerve Chris but he was as distressed as I was. The general sense of desperation coming from all of the people along with the violence that the guy displayed toward the young boy earlier was hard to compute. We just kept saying to each other that we just wanted to leave the place. Every part of the social activity we had seen was hostile and alien to us and swamped our thinking. We arrived at the station which was the same as the rest of the city if not worse. A huge iron and stone dilapidated monster of a building much the same design as a UK station but bigger and run down. There were people everywhere, some literally crawling around with mutilated hands, arms, legs and feet and scared faces with missing eyes and in spaces where they made you wonder how they had got themselves there. We asked the boy why there were so many disabled people to find that generally, the parents mutilate them as babies on purpose so that they attract more pity and so more cash for begging.

In the midst of this depravity and desperation, we had to cash some money for food and to pay for the train tickets. We told the boy we were concerned about being robbed if we were seen going into the bank. He said he would watch out for us and that if the locals saw that we had him around, they wouldn't bother us. Not that he was some 'minder' and would defend us but, that we had him there and were to pay him, at least we were contributing in some way to Calcutta's madness. In saying this it was clear he was experienced with his role, his words were heartfelt and genuine, and he did hold some common protocol that was accepted and followed others. It was the first semblance of humanism we could relate to and without actually thinking it, something we had been searching for since arriving. Now that the boy communicated this, we suddenly felt a little more at ease that they were not all desperate animals.

There were hundreds of people in the station milling around and standing in massively long queues at maybe twenty or more ticket counters. Eventually, through the boy, we found the counter that issued tickets for Delhi and I stood in a line of about thirty or forty people. It took forever so in the meantime Chris took the boy to find some food and water. They came back and we ate and drank, stood for another half hour until eventually it was my turn and the boy told the teller where we were going. We remembered from Hans that the railways gave concessions of 75% off the price. The train ride was about 850 miles so, on discovering that the best fare was about 3 GBP I produced the student union cards. The teller said something and the face of the boy dropped. I could see that he was concerned for us and maybe for himself getting paid as we seem to have discovered a stumbling block in his knowledge and advice. After a few minutes to grasp the meaning through his broken English, although we were in the right line, if we were to use the cards, we had to take the tickets from another counter and stand in another queue. Ugh! It wasn't the boy's fault of course because we hadn't mentioned the cards to him. After around an hour and a half amid the noise of the station and the locals' conversation which amounted to an argument, the smell of sweat and curry, the dry dust lifted in the breeze and smoke from the trains arriving and leaving, we were irritatingly in the wrong place and had to start again. Looking at the queue we were directed to, it appeared to have the same waiting time as the last. We took a little solace from knowing that this was the right one and with some confidence that we were now not so concerned for our safety. The boy was also happy and smiling as we would need him around for a while longer.

After some twenty minutes, the boy went along the line talking to those waiting in front of us and then came back with a bigger smile on his face. He had asked everyone if we could jump the queue as we were going to miss our train if it took too long to stand in line, clearly he was convincing as they had agreed, some begrudgingly. Profusely thanking everyone and feeling a little lighter we collected the tickets for which we paid about 75 pence each which we thought was an absolute coup. Being cautious I had queried the cost and type of seat and if we were to travel on the roof or something but the teller had assured us that we would be in a carriage and would have a seat. With a short time waiting, we walked towards the right platform, paid the boy who was very pleased and explained how he and his whole family were highly delighted. Then boarded the train picking a carriage in the designated class, steerage which at this stage seemed pretty ok, wooden bench seats and a luggage racks on each side. It all looked pretty standard and very bearable.

It was about 6 pm when the train pulled out of Calcutta station, no great announcement we didn't even hear the engine. That was because we were right at the back of a very long train, so we discovered. Before it went dark, we must have stopped two or three times and I thought it must have been because we were still collecting passengers from the suburbs of the city and then, with optimism, we would be off cross country to Delhi. The carriage at this time was full. There were as many people on the luggage racks as there was on the seats, which made 16 of us. It wasn't until we had stopped a few more time that we began to realise that it was to stop almost hundreds of times before we would get to Delhi. After talking to folks, we found out the reason for the cheap tickets was because we were on the milk train and throughout the journey across the virtually the whole of the continent it stopped at every station for the 850 miles taking more than twenty-four hours. Each stop brought changes to those in our carriage and at one point we had another 6 in with us standing on the floor between the seats. The corridor was also full so that it was impossible for people to pass and most of those embarking and disembarking did so through the window followed by the passing from one to another of their luggage. It was a joint effort by all and quite an accepted practice.

We slept where we sat and I think we only ventured out once to pee during the 26 hours. It was hot and dusty through the day with the window open and cold in the night, the smell was almost unbearable when the window was closed. Some of the passengers were very hostile towards us but we held our own and made friends of others. The conversations went from mocking the caste system to how bad we were in the colonial years. We, of course, said that we were not around in those days, so it wasn't our fault or responsibility. Most took the chats in good humour and often the conversation even stretched across scores of miles and changing passengers as they came and went at stations along the way. We woke in the morning as we pulled into yet another station aching from not moving for so long. Hawkers on each new platform would sell patties of some sort of curry, fruits and fruit juice, tea (chia) and water which was very welcome. The conversations continued and most in a relaxed fashion even having the Englishmen with them, flippant about religion and just out to experience different people and places and have fun along the way.

At one stop we took some tea and the seller didn't have milk and we decided to have a lemon. We managed to pay for the tea but we pulled out of the station before we could pay for the lemon. The usual method of the sellers was to go along and serve

110

then they would backtrack to collect the cash. If there were more time, they would go back and do the same again. The train, still packed to the gunnel' with, five or six standing in between the seats, the luggage rack was always full and packed like sardines in the corridor the length of the train. It must have been three or four hours later after lunchtime there was a commotion in the corridor and several in the carriage were laughing. The lemon seller had boarded the train and was shouting at people in the corridor to get out of his way because two Englishmen had robbed him. Thankfully there was still one or two in the carriage that had been there at the time and seen that we were not trying to cheat the guy and it was his fault. He still created and that got the whole carriage involved laughing at the seller and making fun of him. He was so embarrassed that he just left without the cash. We tried to call him back but the other passengers said that he was so nasty about us and they had ridiculed him so badly he wasn't going to come back.

Apart from the stations where we stopped, the view through the window was virtually all of baron countryside. There were a few farms we noticed growing vegetables etc. It was almost impossible to sightsee with so many passengers in the carriage. Some of the company was good and friendly and because we made them laugh, mostly at themselves, they enjoyed our company.

The rest of the trip was quite calm most exchanges after that were more serious than we wanted to deal with so we kept ourselves to ourselves most of the time apart from being courteous in helping people on and off. We managed to sleep a bit as the numbers had reduced to a more normal level with the route through the corridor more passable. We all looked like we had the plague or something. With the heat of the day, we sweated and the dust was around all the time, so all our clothes were virtually rigid like it was a thin coating of cement.

Delhi was a complete contrast to Calcutta. There were similar experiences of poverty and begging but at least here it was interspersed with pretty normal eastern life. Stiff from the journey we found a small hotel in the centre of the city with the help of a tout at the station at a small cost and were inundated with offers to change money. That was good, in the morning we could set off in earnest to sell the cheques. The other major task was to find out if the land border between India and Pakistan (Amritsar/Lahore) was open and somehow find out whether it was worthwhile spending the time by bus or train to find out. The impact of it not being, of course, was the cost of a flight and the next job to find out the nearest and cheapest way of flying if that's what we had to do, or whatever. Food was cheap, pennies for a wholesome Indian meal and the same with the hotel and we could afford to stay a while to work out the best economic route without panicking and choosing a route that led us to a dead end. We talked about going to see the Taj Mahal, we had the time but it was quite a trip and more than we could afford, especially when we would find out how we had to travel from here to cross the border.

We wandered out in the morning and found a small shopping precinct with twenty or thirty shops. Hardly any of them had any goods in the windows. At first, it was a bit of a quandary but it soon became apparent that almost the whole area was for money changers only. We stopped and spoke to several people standing at the doors until we found some that spoke English well and appeared to be as honest as we could make out. Eventually after several cups of tea and sweet snacks time passed and they asked us if we would like some lunch. We both looked sideways and had memories of Hans telling us about being robbed and more faint memories of the purser and his merry men on the ship and we said that we knew there was no such thing as a free lunch. At this point, the central character, pretty fat about 35 years old with a full face beard and turban collapsed with laughter along with his two more quiet colleagues. He said they were going to treat us anyway however sceptical we were and whatever business we do. Suddenly a youth from a café turned up with a tablecloth and utensils and soon after another with all sorts of Indian dishes along with dips and flatbread. They were charming, they bought the cheques and we sold them the watches we had picked up in Singapore. They were very good to us as we explained our situation of having little cash over lunch and they admired us for attempting the trip. That was quite an accolade coming from them as we wouldn't have swapped our dire position with them of living in India for all the tea in…India? We told them we intended to go to Pakistan and then on to Afghanistan, Iran and Turkey etc., and they thought that was very brave. Of course, we didn't have a clue what it was going to be like and only knew that a few other people we had met coming the other way had made it ok and if they had done it…so could we! It was amazing how they took to us and made us feel welcome with the best of intentions so that we left them with a good impression of Indian people after relating the experience in Calcutta.

In a travel agency later that afternoon and from information that we had gathered in the hotel from a couple of other travellers the border was either closed or at best, not something on which to take a chance. For some reason there were no flights into Pakistan; they either were not allowed, or there were no seats for more than a week. The only way we could make progress surely and safely was to fly from Delhi to Kabul in Afghanistan. The blow was that the fights were 100 GBP each, but after once again producing the student union cards stunningly, there was a 60% discount, phew! The drawback was that the first flight did not leave for another three days, so that was another three days of expenses in the same place. Still, there was not a cheaper and surer way of doing this, in fact, no real plausible alternative. All we could do was to settle in and explore a bit of Delhi. At that time wasn't of great interest to us being apprehensive about cash and the realisation of the unknown from Kabul onwards. The apprehension was heightened further when we went back a couple of times to see the money changers and their stories of what we had ahead citing Calcutta as a kindergarten…as if!

However, already we were in the middle of India unscathed and still of good humour and nervously looking forward to the next adventure in the next segment of the trip. There was no choice, we could only keep going, and if the money ran out, we would have to go to the British Embassy, the nearest one and ask them to repatriate us. It sounded good as a backstop, but we still had the fear that they may send us back to Australia. We would cross that bridge when we came to it. For now, we would try to relax and be pleased that we had organised another significant chunk of the trip taking us a few thousand miles nearer Blighty and see if our luck would hold on from there.

-oo-

Palam Airport as it was known then before many years later being named Indira Gandhi International was built by the British during WW2 for use as a Royal Airforce base. As we arrived, it looked like a building site rather than an airport. It was being redeveloped to be four or five times bigger than the original and although most of it was a mess the passenger handling was efficient enough. Still run by the military, the Indian Air Force (was until after the turn of the millennium) as with others we had passed through in the region there was a high military presence. All went well through to the departure lounge and on to the plane, and we lifted off on time. Not quite sure what we were expecting but I can remember us both being pleased that we didn't have any incident or troubles given that we were well aware that anything is possible outside of the UK comfort zone.

The view from the window was quite spectacular as we were skimming the Himalayan chain and even from such a height, the mountains were noticeably more dramatic than any we had seen that went on as far as you could see. The flight was about two hours, and after a small snack of a kind of spicy vegetable pie and a drink, before we knew it, we were descending into Kabul International. A small airport at the time we stepped off the plane and walked to the, fairly small compared to other airports, terminal. The air was electric. It was so sharp, crisp and cold. There was not a cloud in sight, the sun was shining so brightly it made your eyes water. Some 5000 feet above sea level the air was noticeably thin which somehow accentuated the eye-watering soon to be followed by a few sneezes that somehow well up repetitively when in bright sunshine. Each breath felt like it was good for you which made you breath more deeply, clean and healthy. I felt myself wanting to stay there on the tarmac and take it in for a while. It was a complete contrast to the clammy and dusty, warm air of downtown Delhi. It was stark and harsh and exhilarating. Chris had to nudge me to move as he had been standing next to me and everyone else had virtually disappeared into the terminal.

Chapter 9
The Brink of Survival

If you back a cause and then change your mind and go to the opposite side, it takes a lot of deliberation in your mind to justify the change. A northern European moral principle is that you don't. If you make a plan to do something with someone to achieve the goal with help which you depend upon, if they decide to back the opposition it is considered treacherous. Why don't you? As explained in the genius of Winston Churchill of not wasting words yet saying thousands, "A man does what he must – in spite of personal consequences, in spite of obstacles and dangers and pressures, and that is the basis of human morality." It became no surprise that he spent some time on the North Western Front as a young cavalry officer and this is quite possibly where he formed or confirmed these words. Further in fighting the 'wild armoured clansmen', he said it is, "Financially it is ruinous. Morally it is wicked. Militarily it is an open question, and politically it is a blunder."

In this area of the world, morality isn't so cut and dried. Why this is an acceptable practice takes some figuring while cosily sitting by the fire having eaten a large Sunday lunch and finishing off with fruit salad and cream in the afternoon in England. It does not take long in this, a very different environment to see that those who do switch sides do have a point, like it or not. It is not a free ticket to being flippant and uncaring to do what you like arbitrarily; it goes much deeper than that. It's a result of a continual consequence of dealing with life on a life or death basis daily and not a decision between choosing Tesco-owned brand or McVities Digestives. There it is so tough that all the time you must reassess your circumstances and re-plan taking into account the best options for the best chance of survival. It's not until you are there, experiencing the severe conditions and circumstances under which those decisions made that a deeper understanding of why they feel it necessary and acceptable to switch. Afghanistan is one of those places. A strategic key to east-west travel from the days of Genghis Kahn, the Persians, India and Alexander the Great through many others to occupation by the British in the early nineteenth and twentieth centuries, Russians in the late 1970s and more recently Allied forces of the USA and Europe.

Generally, their demeanour is raw and wild with the people living in severe conditions all the time. In part through history, as Churchill doubtlessly found, their plight was exaggerated by the forerunners of the Taliban. A sect called the Talib-ul-ilms ("of their morals and manners it is impossible to write" in Churchill's words), a rough group of pseudo holy men that lived off the goodwill and hospitality of the people, subjugating the Afghan tribes through controlling superstitions. And herein lays a tale. No doubt this part of their history had made them tough with meagre lives having little to give but still taken advantage of over many years by their people. We arrived in Kabul, unbeknown to us, a few days before their New Year; the festivities bring hosts of people out of the wilderness to the celebrations in and around the city. It was wild; we just assumed they acted like this all the time. What a place! It wasn't until we remarked about the antics that we were informed it was a special time. We didn't know how wild it was during the rest of the year, but now it made more sense that it was somewhat wilder now because of the special celebrations where they let their hair down.

Outside the hotel, they seemed to be playing a game of chicken or a duel of some kind in the roads outside the hotel riding horses at each other wielding lances or poles of some sort and swerving to one side at the last moment and viciously lashing out at their opponent. Spectators and or just passing by onlookers on boardwalks would cheer as both horses skidded and almost fell over on the swerve in the mud of the street. Wow! We were too speechless and too frightened that we may have been roped into one of these bouts if we had cheered. It was the sort of game you may see played out on the television in village locations in the countryside, but this was in the capital city, the business centre of the country where people sat in suits in offices and discussed supply and demand and taxes etc., or so we assumed. We were not in that district of the city, or maybe we were? They had done it before and were completely involved in it and themselves. I remember wondering if they knew each other from before and just met up at these celebrations to batter each other near to death and it was their display of friendship albeit a little severe. We had found it a challenge and made it a purpose on our travels of trying to attract locals' attention, but these guys were difficult; they were not to be distracted from their 'fun'. Taking in this spectacle at that moment, nor did we want to try!

Throughout all of this display, verging on abject violence, there was still a vein of respect for each other. Although it could be that accidentally the tribesmen may kill one another I'm sure it would all have been in the pursuance of camaraderie and they would have given the most unfortunate a decent burial, drunk something that would make them more wild and awake back in their villages without a single recollection of what happened. That was the problem with being among them. Their games should have had a public warning pinned to their backs 'this shit is fatal!' Thank goodness we had been ignored or dismissed since we arrived there, at least they wouldn't ask us to get involved and die in the process. It may seem like an exaggeration, but it isn't! Looking back now, that must have been where the uneasiness came from that was so hard to fathom and describe. These guys were off the wall for fun with their antics just as they were off the wall with the severity of their every day, on the edge of survival lives…this was their version of fun, up in the mountains on the top of the world.

Charging around on the horses, they seemed like armed and wearing wild bears. They even looked like wild bears, adorned in fur coats with fur hats and boots and braids of ammunition crossed on their chests like bandits. I remember thinking they probably were bandits! Our stay in Kabul was short, less than 24 hour due to expedience rather than fear but I am not sure what we would have made out of the place if we had stayed longer given our circumstances. It was still fascinating probably because we still hadn't managed to connect in the slightest with anyone. No one escapes us ultimately but what would it take and when would we have enough balls to try. A few times we just looked at each other and without saying a word subconsciously decided to leave it for another time when we thought we might be able to get away with it…..with our lives intact. We did have our 'other guest' in the hotel room laughing later that evening, but we couldn't assume anything, he could well just have been completely nuts as he didn't turn to us after and say, 'that was funny'.

It was not until many years later that I found the Churchill words in some reading. After going about life, past experiences kind of trundle along in the background if you haven't completely understood or processed situations comfortably. Then something reminds you of them which instantly and vividly flashes back to mind, and his words did exactly that. Through our experience, being there and seeing it, I couldn't help but agree with and develop a more thorough understanding. Not quite sure of the value of such thinking but at the very least it confirmed a similar 'Britishness' in common with a distinguished Brit. Having mulled over the severity of life where someone else had the same opinion, irrespective that our experience was some eighty years later, that explained it in one. However, although our circumstances didn't involve fighting a war and a life or death situation that needed their full-hearted co-operation, I could still not help but admire their tenacity in coping with life there.

-oo-

It only took a few minutes from the hotel to the bus station. We felt very isolated as we boarded the bus and sat behind a very short rotund Frenchman who was speaking French to the Afghani next to him which someway eased our self-imposed alienated apprehension. I thought it unusual but then thought how good it was for the fully robed local to speak French. Later we found that he didn't speak a word and the Frenchman was a little crazy. Suddenly we heard the German voices, and as we turned around, there was Gunther and Hans. Gunther being fatherly ushered along the bus by Hans. From our conversations in Bangkok, they had been planning to travel a similar route back to Europe, but we didn't expect to meet them so soon. After we thought it probably was quite timely as we had been delayed in Delhi, of course, waiting for the next flight. They had been in

Kabul for a couple of days as they flew from Bangkok straight to Delhi, missing out Calcutta purposely as Hans had been there before and knew it for what it was. I remember Hans in the hotel in Bangkok telling us about it, but there was something with the flight tickets from there. Maybe in the mix and match it was the best route for the discount to apply and timing or similar. He and Gunther were not as restricted as we were with cash as Gunther had access to cash through his mother back in Oz or his father in Germany.

That hop saved them another couple of days as they didn't overnight in Rangoon as we did. It was a coincidence to meet anyone even though we were on a similar route; this was long before mobile phones.......half the time in the middle of nowhere and the other half in the middle of the mountains. You couldn't just give them a quick call to see where they were. Not what is done today where you may speak twenty times and spend as much time on the phone beforehand as the time you spend together when you meet. Still, it was a welcome surprise to see them; the whole bus was full of Afghanis apart from us four and the Frenchman. All were quite aware that we were friends as we made a fuss of them when they boarded, and that made us feel a little easier. We kept ourselves to ourselves taking in the deep snow covered scenery. All the locals were bearded and dressed in plain greyish Mujahidin/Taliban type robes, some with dark jackets and the typical round flat cap. Some wore a brown or black turban; very few of them had any conversation not even with each other, mostly just sat in silence and looked serious.

We left the city and were soon out into the wilderness with literally no sign of other life apart from wildlife. Now a highway but then it was just a smallish winding ill-maintained road, a goodly part with no tarmac, just stone compacted by the traffic usage. In some parts, we drove slowly over snow for long stretches at a time. It must have been gruelling for the driver as it was terrifying many times over for us with steep mountains to climb and descend with sheer cliff faces to one side and just as sheer drops to the other. The route took us through to the south part of the Hindu-Kush Mountains with breathtaking snow-covered scenery for at least 400 km and very cold for most of the way. The whole journey to Kandahar, which was the only way through Afghanistan, was about 500 km and a little under

119

halfway to where we were to cross the border near the town of Herat to go into Persia to a town called Mashed.

So after this mammoth trip, we had the same again through the end of the mountain range. Kandahar is near the southern tip of the Kush range, no roads and impassable on a straight line through the middle of the country any further north than Kandahar. It wasn't until we neared the city that the dramatic mountain road levelled out and the temperature began to rise noticeably. From being high in the mountains with snow and very cold to the lowlands more akin to dessert and fairly warm. Although nerve-racking it was exhilarating, it was sunny all the day, but for a few snow showers where it was darkish and still, we stopped at a kind of shop halfway through the day to have some food and a drink. In the evening as it was going dark, we stopped for an overnight stay where we slept for a while on wooden benches in one big room. The luggage was locked in the bus. The roads were bad in the daytime but dangerously impossible at night because of the conditions and the possibility of bandits. Although it was all still the one country of Afghanistan, we passed through areas that were governed by completely different tribes and cultures that were not necessarily at peace with one another. Even though after the nerve-wracking five or six hours to the first stop we wanted the journey to be over we were pleased about stopping overnight with those prospects in mind. At each stop, we spent time with Gunther and Hans where he would tell us about his experiences when he was there last. All very useful he prepared us for being in Kandahar which is a fundamental religious centre where the locals were far more serious, he said we should not make eye contact and avoid any interaction outside of doing what we needed to do in fixing the next part of the trip.

We climbed into the bus having woken and had tea with some bread which we paid little for after some arguing with the owner of the stopover facilities. We climbed onto the bus as there was some shouting with the Frenchman deeply involved with the kind of bus conductor. They were shouting at one another; I thought that the Afghani who the Frenchman was sitting next to who we thought he had been in conversation with would have helped him out. We had misread this friendship, we had the wrong idea altogether so couldn't understand why there wasn't support for the Frenchman. We must have seemed aggressive coming out in support of the Frenchman, and suddenly the bus conductor pulled out a knife and gestured that he was going to stab the Frenchman. Chris stood up and went forward in the aisle, and the conductor took a step back as I was halfway out of my seat and pushing the Frenchman back down in his seat when I saw that he also had a knife which neither of us saw at first. The difference was that originally he was using it to peel an apple. The conductor probably would have killed us all. Because we stood up, he must have thought twice about being so upfront himself. I was also holding back the Frenchman who was now less of a threat. Chris told the guy a couple of times to put the knife away, the Frenchman stayed sat down, and conductor reluctantly turned away and sheathed the knife. We then turned to the Frenchman and asked him what the problem. It was all over his cycle on the roof. He had some items in the bag fastened to it that he wanted and the conductor wouldn't get it from him. Chris gestured asking how much to do this, and the conductor laughed as if to say that we now understood what the Frenchman didn't. Some moments after and before we got on our way again the conductor came back on the bus with the bag in his hand and passed it to the Frenchman. He didn't take any money.

So, there we were on a bus in Afghanistan full of Afghanis with two Germans and an uppity Frenchman that appeared to be threatening the conductor and we stepped into the middle of it. Thank goodness for that bit of humour from Chris that seemed to turn the mood. I think that the conductor also saw that we as Europeans, having seen that the Frenchman had a knife, appreciated that we didn't just leap to his side and defend him, we just wished to bring all back from the brink of trouble and settle the dispute in some way without blood. It broke the ice, and each time the conductor came by, now not feeling threatened, he nodded in guarded appreciation. The incident influenced the other passengers who now at the very least acknowledged our existence after this event for the rest of the journey. We did also run the risk of being roped into one of their crazy games now we were friends, which would have been a bit of a worry, but we just hoped we wouldn't get so close. In the next partway stop for fuel and water the conductor brought us tea. We said how about the Frenchman; he looked as if to say, now you are taking the piss. We chuckled and sat with him until we finished the tea. By now we realised that the Frenchman was quite crazy, he had just been prattling all the time with the Afghani to his annoyance without any understanding at all. The Afghani badgered by the Frenchman must have complained to the conductor, and there started the aggravation and standoff before our involvement. The conductor could see that we were trying to be level-headed and showed his appreciation. The first connection we had made with these life-hardened people and a very welcome connection it was.

The rest of the trip to Kandahar went without event. As we went through a very remote area of vast snowfields with mountains as the backdrop there were wolves or large wolf-like wild dogs chasing a fox, and all the passengers were cheering on the wolves. As we gradually lost altitude, the snow disappeared, and within a short distance, the surroundings now were dry and warm. We felt pretty good at having made a 'friend' of the conductor and had some recognition from other passengers, and now it was warmer we were looking forward to a good night's sleep with a lot of anxiety being a thing of the past. We said our goodbyes to our new 'friends' as we stepped down from the bus. Hans knew a hotel which Gunther and he and we headed to.

-oo-

We had a spring in our step after the bus incident, and when we got to the hotel, Hans sat us down and reminded us of the fundamental nature of the district. It seemed that he now had some problem with us after the event on the bus. We quizzed him and he said that we should do as we were asked. Not exactly the most intelligent thing to say. We appreciated his help with all the information and advice that had been of immense value information wise and financially with the discount cards etc., and we had given him respect for that, but laying down the law in that way didn't rest easy with us. He was vehement about us taking his lead and not making any contact with the locals. We had just done much to make a connection, from which he had benefited as we had made it obvious that all four of us were travelling companions. He still didn't like the idea that we had this connection and said that if we were not to do as he said, almost not speak unless he said so, he didn't want us to be associated with him and Gunther because he thought we would cause trouble. Of course, that didn't stack with us; we told him that it was his choice. He didn't even want to stay in the same hotel with us after he could see we basically disagreed and he and Gunther were going to find a different hotel. We said that he should not take it all to heart. After all, we were not going around causing trouble, quite the opposite as on the bus we had stopped the trouble. Surely that was good, and he could see how the conductor reacted by bringing the tea and sitting with us. Hans thought that it was not good enough, but Gunther was torn over the incident. I remember thinking that Hans was at this stage overly protective of Gunther. Our attitude with him was, yes he needed a bit of supervision as in the incident on the ship, but he was ok and could look after himself. Looking for a motive, I thought about the access to funding from Gunther's mother or father and wondered if their withdrawal was a scheme from Hans in a combination of his protectiveness and jealousy coupled with Hans's need for support from Gunther more than the other way around. If we were right, it was irksome the way that Gunther was being manipulated, and we were being made out to be wrong. Being in such surroundings and such severe circumstances makes you think more deeply because of the consequences of your choices. It sharpens your critical path analysis abilities and highlights any untoward motives that don't quite fit a clean development of thought to formulate the best way forward. It was one of those ill-fitting times. We did feel that we hadn't found a wholesome reason for this mood shift, if we had, we would have been able to overcome it. Overall it seemed very divisive. Hans sunk on the scale of respect from then and there was very little that we could say or do. Hans had the family connection with Gunther which would have taken some considerable thought and explanation to discredit him. However, although we had some concern, it wasn't our problem to resolve. It was Gunther's choice and he made it, we left it at that and we parted.

We mulled over the disagreement as they left. Apart from the information about places and the route etc., we had spent very little time with them actually in transit. We suspected it was a jealousy thing. Gunther had thought a lot of us in the first place from looking after him on the ship. Hans could see he had time for us as in conversation he was always speaking well of us and bolstering our points. He was a good, open-hearted kid and that was why we spent time thinking the best for him. As we had gained some respect from the conductor and the other passengers it seemed that it took the light from Hans. Gunther knew that we had a good manner when there was trouble and possibly this was a little threatening to Hans. It didn't matter as we were ok anyway so after spending some time between us pulling the event apart we drew a line, found some food and went back to the hotel room and slept early. They didn't take the bus onto Herat the next day, and we never saw them again and still never really figured out what had happened.

-oo-

We had only been in the country some 48 hours and most of it in very cold weather, so it was pleasant wakening in the relative warmth. Still not the most secure of places to sleep over with a curtain as a door again but this time it just went out into the street, no one disturbed us in the night. We were up in enough time to have tea and water and some bread due once again to our lifesaver, Chris' alarm clock, before it was time to board the bus to Herat. We had gained a lot of confidence strength from the exchanges of yesterday and still had some spring in our step. That's why we were perplexed about how Hans had belittled what had happened. It was disappointing that we had a different conductor and driver, a different, smaller bus. The one from Kabul was already on its way back to fulfil its twice a week schedule, and we were now on the western service. It took longer on the way back up to Kabul.

This part of the journey didn't have any significant 'events' at all which was fine with us. It was almost boring, but there was still some rugged countryside, mostly desert type until we had travelled for a few hours northwest where we were back in the mountainous zone but only for a short while. We did sleep a lot because the road conditions were that much better than the trip to Kandahar. The route was over lower and flatter ground generally and it was less dramatic and much quicker even though it was slightly further by road than that the previous leg of the journey. Overall it took less time to do an additional 100 km as this road was less dangerous and so reaching our destination was easily doable without an overnight stop. We had a refreshments stop and from the early start, we arrived in Herat in the early evening. There is a 'no man's land' between the Afghani and Iranian borders through which you can only travel by bus or car of course. We all got off the bus which was to wait for a couple of hours while all the travellers went through the checkpoints of customs and immigration. It was here where things were about to take a turn for the worst.

We were buoyant from how much we had gained from the country after thinking that was wasn't a hope in hell of doing so. After the good sleep in Kandahar and some hours napping while on the bus to Herat. That was us rested and refreshed. The border post was an isolated building with no shops or any other building around. Towards Iran over the 'no man's land,' it was a rocky with dried scrub bushes like a desert area. We stood in the long slow queue to do the official stuff and first there was customs. The officials were not in uniform, the one in our line in the distance wore just jeans with a tweed type jacket. The shoulder split open and some of the stuffing exposed.

After 15 or 20 minutes it was our turn. In broken English, he asked if we had anything to declare and we, of course, said no. Just then the alarm clock in Chris' bag went off. He quickly took it out and switched it off and as the guy was already emptying the bag left it on the counter. After rummaging around the officer asked if it was his clock and picked it up examining it. Chris, of course, said yes. It obviously took his fancy and he commented how nice it was. Chris looked at me and back at the officer who then asked if he could have the clock. It was a normal clock with the 2 bells on the top, the cheapest you could buy. Chris looked over again and we both chuckled. It was kind of quaint and we thought that the guy was taking the mickey. Chris said, "We use it every day to get up in time to catch buses and trains and flights as we had done for the last number of weeks, what would we do if we did not have one?" Thinking that that would end the leg pull he started to put his things back in the bag. The officer stopped him. We asked what the problem was. Again, the officer said it's a nice clock can I have it? Thinking he was still joking Chris said, "No I'm sorry you can't, it's a family air loom. My father would never speak to me again if I gave it away." The officer glared at him and started to put Chris' stuff back in the bag. We thought, thank goodness for that, that's us through, but the guy finished and said we should wait over to one side. Immediately he turned to the next person in line. We stood for a minute and then went toward the way out. The officer went mad and called another policeman over. He said he told us to go and wait and we must do this.

Suddenly we realised his seriousness and had no alternative but to do as they said as the policeman ushered us to a waiting area. We sat for around an hour, both of us were showing our disapproval and we gestured over to the officer that we were still there that he could not have the clock and we were going to miss our bus. He ignored us. All the goodwill we had created with the conductor and the Frenchman was disappointingly starting to fall apart and that uneasiness was starting to return. Another half hour went by and we were wound up at the injustice. Just because we wouldn't give……an official a personal item, he was holding up our journey and now we were in danger of missing the bus which we had to take to cross into Iran.

We made the decision that we had waited for long enough and picked up the bags and walked over to him. Chris said, "Look we haven't anything to declare and now we are going to catch the bus." He said he wanted to look at our passports. As soon as we handed them over, he went into the back office by which time we were livid, and Chris shouted, "You can't have the alarm clock, and that's the end of it," thinking that the embarrassment would make him let us go. He then threatened to arrest us if we were not quiet. Just as we were just about to raise the ante and probably land ourselves in deeper trouble an English girls voice came from the back saying, "Please be calm, these men are English, and they don't understand the ways and customs of such a proud nation." She was about 23/4 and good looking girl about 5'5", blond hair in a kind of bob style in jeans and denim shirt. We certainly did know now the antics and the customs, of the customs. We were about to pile in again when she told us to be quiet and listen to the officer. Something had changed the guy's mind; another ranking officer had come into the area on hearing the commotion. It must have been his boss as a glance from him, and he was signalling to the girl that he was backing down and going to let us through. Very quickly he handed our passports back and allowed us to pass. "Phew," said Chris.

"Phew," said the girl, "You don't know what the hell these guys can put you through if you get on the wrong side of them. They are ruthless, and it's a good job I was there to calm the officer." We were still not in a mood to be calm but listened to her as we then headed toward immigration. She had a way with her and the customs guy did take notice of her. We calmed and thanked her and introduced ourselves; she was called Anne. Chris says, "Well whatever, we won, we still have the alarm clock."

We still had a wait to clear immigration; the bus driver had already been into the building looking for us saying that he had to leave. Fortunately, so we then find out, there are other buses all the time. Although we felt it to be a bit of security that the driver had waited for us, it wasn't a problem that we didn't cross on this same bus we had taken from Kandahar. Well, we were not to know, part of our panic in trying to get through customs was the urgency of the bus having to leave. 'What on earth are you doing here in the middle of nowhere and on your own', I say. 'I'm not on my own, I have a boyfriend and we also have another girl travelling with us. We have some things to do and then by the time you have finished here we will be in the car park across from the post office as you enter Mashed, the town just over the border in Iran, come and meet us there when you have finished and caught the next bus'.

Well, after all the fuss we were clear, it took a while to get by immigration, we waited some 30 minutes for the next bus to leave which seemed like a lifetime, no one was happier than us to have that whole experience behind us. And we are off to meet some English if we could find them, the first for thousands of miles, and the girl although she had said she was with a boyfriend, she gave me the impression that she was a bit sweet on me. Optimistically this was looking like another phoenix situation in the making, in what fashion we didn't know. We had no idea how much of a phoenix this million to one chance meeting would be.

Afghanistan was an experience, and although the border event was stressful, we were pleased that at least we were able to connect with some people who from first impressions of the people we didn't hold out any hope of finding a human communicative side to them. It was important to us just as with the money changers in Delhi, even the boy in Calcutta who came through in the end, the spitting stewardess in Rangoon who was rather cute if you discount her disgusting habits and the people in Thailand and Malaya who showed us so much hospitality and consideration. With each of them we pushed out the boat, and although in some instances it took some time, they opened up and warmed to us too.

Our major looming problem was the shortage of cash. By this time we were not so much thinking about being repatriated. Having come so far, although it was only a possibility that we would be shipped off back to Australia, we didn't want to take the chance. As we crossed Afghanistan, we were thinking more regarding getting to Turkey and having my father……………or Chris's cable some money to us. Singapore had been unreliable, and Afghanistan was even worse as far as having organised commercial systems in place, and we could only guess that Iran would be similar. We didn't know exactly, but we just had the idea that Turkey would be the best bet. If we could get to there with the stash we had, the princely sum of 40 pounds between us, maybe at least we could get someone back home to organise tickets from say Istanbul to the UK. Of course, that was still a dream as we had some 4000 kilometres to do before that could be a way forward. It was a test of our resolve and probably the biggest one to date.

-oo-

It was now dark and about 9.30pm, with these daunting financials in front of us we stepped on to the bus to cross into Iran. It wasn't too inspiring to think about the money. So, what do we do when we start having thoughts we are not comfortable with? We put it right out of our minds and think about something else; suddenly remembered that we had made an arrangement to meet with the English girl Anne and her friends over the Iranian border in Mashed. There you go, it worked, our thinking was comfortable again! Back to my mind came the car park opposite the post office Anne had described. Startlingly, as we approached the town, standing at the door by the driver in a massive coincidence, there it was next to the bus stop. We were exactly where we needed to be. We walked into the car park looking for them and an English car, and there it was. There was a kind of homely feeling came over us. After all the trials and tribulations and thousands of kilometres we had gone through over the last weeks in places and environments that were alien to us and in no way related to anything British, there was an English registered VW camper. I couldn't help it; I hugged Anne as if she was a long lost friend irrespective of the fact that we had only met for a few minutes less than a couple of hours ago. We sat for ages talking about where we had been and what we had done, we had them in stitches. After a while we said that we must find a hotel and they said there was one next door to the car park, was very cheap, open all the time and always had beds of sorts. Well said Chris that was the next part of the plan in place, all we had to do was find a way of getting by the next 4000 kilometres. They made some food, and soon they were telling us how they had ended up there and what they were doing.

The guy Bob was with Anne; they lived together in the UK. The other girl Christine was the girlfriend of their absent friend. They didn't say where the absent friend was. We could feel there was some reluctance, as they got that far with the story, as to whether or not to tell us anymore. Although their reluctance didn't register at first, it was just a hunch as we were tucking into the food and wine. It came back to mind, and we became puzzled and curious as to what could be so sinister that they couldn't tell us. Putting that aside, they asked how we had planned to reach England or Istanbul as we had made mention of flying back from there. We told them the plan of maybe a ticket sent from the UK or being repatriated by the embassy if that was possible. The risk with that plan involved the possibility of being sent back to Australia. Anne then said, "Look, we are going back to the UK anyway, we are short of cash so if we liked they would take us." We looked at each other in disbelief. Chris said, "Would you mind repeating that, I think I might have misheard you." She continued saying that it would work out ok for them too as we would contribute to the expenses for fuel and food. As soon as she mentioned money, we both had a sinking feeling as we were just about to stumble into the problem; all we had was 40 pounds.

We said that could be a bit difficult because we didn't have so much cash. "How much do you have," said Anne. At this point, we laughed as we knew full well no one would believe us, 40 pounds to travel the best part of 8000 ms? Chris, looking rather sheepish as he could see this whole miracle that had just been promised, collapse and disappear for the rest of our lives said, "Forty pounds."

"But we have a lot of optimism!"

They laughed and Anne said, "Well, that sort of bullshit it's going to make it fun if we are to spend a lot of time close together." Uncontrollably we laughed because we knew it was true.

Those last few words 'if we are going to spend a lot of time close together' hung in my mind like a dream come true. It wasn't that I was besotted with her, although she was quite tasty, it was the thought of the trip back being arranged all in one go. Then our stark reality came back to mind. I say, "It's true, we wish it weren't, but it is!" At that point we all started laughing; Bob gathered himself together, and deadly straight, still convinced we were not telling the truth said, "Well this is going to be fun with you two jokers if you can tell such porkies." That did it, by this time both of us were rolling on the floor with the three of them staring at us. I say, "We wouldn't have believed us either." It took some more minutes for the next bout of laughter to subside and to convince them that was where we were at. "We will both strip to our underpants, and you can search all our clothes and bags. You won't find another penny," says Chris. "I'd even take off my underpants for a financial consideration given our predicament."

More raucous laughter followed both of us waiting for one of them to say, "Go on then."

As we were relating the story, under their breath, they just kept saying, "How the fuck?" They stared at us in amazement and couldn't grasp that we were there with so little money. Neither could we if started to think of it. So, all in all, their reaction was quite understandable and probably how we would have reacted ourselves, the boot being on the other foot. Having travelled from England across Turkey and Iran on the way there and knew what was in front of us and thought that it was blatantly not enough to survive. By now it was around midnight, and we said we had better go to the hotel. The opportunity had passed us by, and Chris said we ought to leave, and we would see them before they went on their way in the morning.

I didn't know why exactly at the time but it was late. We were devastated, completely gutted. As we were walking to the hotel Chris said that Anne had taken a strong shine to me and Bob started to notice. He had a second sense with these things, what that meant could be that it was a strong enough attraction so she could want us to go with them irrespective of the lack of cash. I say, "Since when did you elect yourself as my pimp, selling my body for a lift?"

"No time to suddenly pull an out of character moral stance," both of us chuckled, "if there is a chance of them taking us on board, which this way there could be, let's just see how it develops in the morning." Right now it was an absolute outsider and we were not building up our hopes but now feeling a little better having this last chance in mind'. We checked in and paid with a bit of Afghan money we had, about 10 pence and went to sleep saying that, whether we got the lift which on and off seemed preposterous, or not we could manage whatever happened. We were not in any worse situation than before we met them. Anne was good with the customs officer problem but I'm sure we would have backed down from that anyway.

The morning was overcast, and we bought some water and wandered into the car park. Bob and Anne had gone to buy some things for breakfast, and Christine said we should wait and at least eat with them. They came back, and we had boiled eggs and bread and a cup of Tetley's tea. Chris and I were preparing ourselves mentally to go. Just sitting there with the English and having breakfast they made for us was lulling us into a false sense of security. We knew it was going to be difficult to make it back on our own and thinking about what could have been wasn't going to fill us with the strength to achieve it. We did think that we could call the UK and see if we could have some cash sent that we could give them. Chris said that we might as well take the chance as we were. If our folks were to bail us out, we might as well take it for a flight as we had no guarantee that the trip with the English would work out. Anything could happen, with no making from any of us. If something went awry, then where would we be? We couldn't call for more for a flight from wherever we got to with them. They could see the logic in what we were saying. After all, although they had not given us the full story of how the other one of the original four wasn't still with them, clearly they were off their original plan so something had gone wrong with them so we all knew, 'anything could happen'.

We started to move. Just then Anne chirps up, "Look, we have more of a story to tell you. You think you have troubles? We set off from the UK as two couples and had the vehicles specially prepared to have compartments to stash a quantity of hashish to take back to the UK," We both sat upright thinking that they still didn't believe us about the amount of money we had so now they were bullshitting us. Chris said smiling, 'ok you have got us back we ought to leave to let you smoke yourselves daft about our struggle to get home'.

Anne said, "No it's not bullshit," which made us start laughing again. "James, Christine's boyfriend, loaded up and set off from Pakistan to Afghanistan which is the easiest border of all as a test on his own, and the people from whom he bought the drugs from informed the customs. Of course, he denied it, but the customs officer said that he knew what he had and if he was to give him $5000 he could go free." We were still both stunned as she went on. "So, being put off by the bad luck in what we are doing after this setback, we are going back home to raise the money to get him out. He is being held hostage without his passport in the customs officer's house."

"Pretty fantastic," says Chris, "I thought we were good, but you make us sound like children."

"No wait until I've finished," Anne says. "As you can imagine this has caused us a lot of upheavals and to do a lot of thinking, Bob and I are at each other's throats and have been since leaving the UK, being so close to one another for so long has made things even worse. Christine is fraught and worried about James. We had such a relaxing time with you two last night, the first time we had laughed in months and especially now that James is unable to move from here we are even tenser, we think you would be good company, and we would like you to come with us." Our scheme discussed last night as we went to the hotel wasn't panning out exactly the way we thought, it was even better. Chris, not wanting to believe what we heard just yet, says, "What about the money, or the lack of it?"

Christine cut in and said, "At least it's a bit extra so long as you don't eat it all away in food, it is going to contribute even though it is not much. Even if you do, you are still a good company and have brought us some hope that the journey back will be easier and more enjoyable. We will be happy to take you with us."

"You must be prepared for some attention on the trip because we don't know if we might be stopped having been involved in the failed attempt and don't know if the customs might inform these here in Iran but we don't think so," said Anne.

Bob says, "And I want you to help with the driving, Christine doesn't, and Anne is not happy driving so it will give me a break and take some of the responsibility from me too. It's not easy one bloke travelling with two young women for several reasons."

They were genuinely pleased to see us when they came back with the food for breakfast. After we ate, all along as we were talking through these last few minutes I was sensing what was coming and I had been pinching myself and nudging Chris. Now it was confirmed, and it was still difficult to take in. On the bones of our asses, next to no money, 7000 km away from home with the prospect of being shipped back to Australia someone offered us a lift all the way back with nothing else to pay but the little cash we had. Chris says, "Absolutely not, do you think we are fools!" Everyone choked laughing, and of course, we agreed and thanked them profusely. We gave them the cash, and they went off to buy some supplies, and we walk around for an hour taking in the first taste of Persia. We could not believe the luck. We certainly were blessed, and a huge weight had gone from our shoulders. All the time we had been talking I noticed Anne looking at me, she was giving me more attention than I expected, that could be a problem with Bob no matter how many previous problems they admitted. Something I must watch to keep things good between us all. What a trip and what a turn up for the books, if you told the story no one would believe it. The only real worrying obstacle we were constantly dealing with had been taken away at a stroke; we just had to deal with the circumstances on the ground each day as we had until now. We knew there would still be many trials and tribulations to deal with but the big one of how we were going to get there was done and organised, we just had to keep things sweet. And Chris didn't have to sell my body, although the overall prospect of getting together with Anne was becoming more appealing. Unbelievable squared then unbelievable cubed.

Chapter 10
Listening but Not Looking

Both of us being a little forceful, we had to be careful to keep the balance and not be overbearing with our new found friends and co-travellers. Right from that miraculous morning, we were probably the luckiest two people across both hemispheres and from that moment in time we kept reminding ourselves just how lucky we were. For me, they could do or say anything so long as they took us with them. They were also entertaining and open, our light-hearted view of life seemed to bring them out of themselves. They were good people in their own right and from the outset we got along. From the first day, I don't remember a time when the atmosphere between us was strained near to a point where the relationships were damaged. It was no great effort to keep that going. In our outrageously good fortune, it was not a drudge for them, they genuinely liked us and enjoyed our company, and both of us intended to keep it that way. I guess their task was a gruelling trip with no prize after their initial plan was with a good win out of their trip. Now they had all the same work to do with the prize of losing, in fact paying. When their spirits were low and were depressed at the prospect of what they had to do to solve their problems we lifted them with our attitude, strength and humour. Paradoxically they had done something similar with us, we were not depressed but knew we had a steep hill to climb to get to England. Although we had formulated a couple of ways to get over this, they were not the best of solutions, having to be bailed out after all the effort we made to get so far to date. Now the daunting prospect of having to figure something out based on a severe lack of cash had gone. We didn't have that buzzard circling over our heads waiting for a point where we had nothing.

Apart from bringing a completely contrasting fresh outlook to the trip, it meant that as we were doing some of the driving, they were able to make better progress and ultimately get back sooner or with less effort on their part. We were as happy as we could be with getting exactly what we needed, a lift back to the UK and didn't mind the driving in the least. Additionally, for their part, one guy travelling through hostile and dangerous places with two young good looking English girls was a huge responsibility for Bob. With us along the numbers were completely different and much of that strain and stress was off him. It worked even better, for good or for bad relationships wise as Anne and I were a little attracted to one another. There was resentment in Bob but that was a result of whatever happened before we came along. I can't remember exactly what, but in discussion with Christine sometime later there had been some major bust-up with Christine present and from what was said then, she knew it was fatal.

Christine was worried about James most of the time. It was hard to imagine being held hostage in some strangers' house and locked for most of the time in the attic, that stranger was a government official…a customs officer at that! There was little wonder that Christine spent a lot of her time being tearful. We were always trying to bring her round saying that whatever it was that she thought, it would make no difference to what was happening to him and he would be looked after because he meant money to the customs guy. She had been to the house and seen his circumstances. Also, she had met the customs guy and over the course of a week or so got to know his family. By this stage, although not under ideal circumstances, the daily course of events was by consensus rather than by force and under duress. Just going over the past events helped her cope when she was missing him. Now and then Chris would take the bull by the horns and say something like, "Thinking about it, it could be worse."

Startled Christine asked, "How the hell do you work that one out?"

"Well, it could be me, I could be the prisoner," as Chris throws his head in the air, I'd known him for many years and knew where he was going.

"Yes but you are only thinking of yourself, how does that make it any better?" Chris says.

"Yes I know I am, for me that would be a lot worse than how it is, even worse it could be you there, would that be worse?" Eventually, Christine had to admit that of course, it would be worse for her if she was the prisoner.

"That's what I mean; it could be worse. Granted it doesn't make it better for him, but if it were worse for you, you would not be involved in solving the problem for him, and where would that leave him?" All this was pretty obvious but Chris saying what was obvious made them think that, given the circumstances, they were doing what was needed to solve the problem and no amount of worry was going to change that or improve what was happening. The interlude was a way of getting past a low moment, it worked and Chris felt pleased with himself.

It became obvious to all that Anne and I had something going on. Bob was patently as aware of this as all were. They had been going through a lot of trouble even back in the UK and had pretty much decided then that they were to split after they came back from this trip. It was going to be their way of being able to part as the original plan with the cash they would make. Now that wasn't the case they had the task of parting without money, and they had to find the cash to release James. I started to feel much better rather than me just thinking that Anne was taking advantage of Bob and in turn, I was too. Their relationship wasn't my problem, and I did not want to be involved in influencing how it would go regarding whether they would stay together or not. Both she and Christine explained where she and Bob had got to with their relationship when they could see I was nervous about Anne's attention and from there on we all communicated better.

It took a couple of days before we finally stopped pinching ourselves about the degree of luck in securing the journey home. Even though from Singapore we had the worry of money or the lack of it, we were buoyant as these three had experienced from us on the first evening we met. After a while it became what was happening rather than a miraculous stroke of luck (although it still was), the reality of their situation started to sink in with us. Although we were flippant about our encounter at the Afghan

Iranian border, we knew that things could go wrong fairly rapidly. With them and their task, having been caught out, one of them being held hostage.........by the authorities (which left little to say about their Afghan authority) and further to have a demand for payment to release the guy was a huge lump to digest. They now had to go back to the UK, find the money...and then go out again! We were upset merely at them wanting an alarm clock; they must have been beside themselves at having to find and bring back thousands of a ransom. It did rather highlight the seriousness of their plight and put it into perspective. It was on their minds continually but us being generally insouciant with life was a lift to their spirits, and as we were thanking them, they were thanking us. After a while, we just accepted that it was good for all of us. We should cease being grateful to one and other and get on with it. That made us all feel ok.

It was a kind of bliss but boring just sitting in the van as we were driving. We had spent the last weeks continually sorting out the plan of where we were going and how, we almost missed the nerve-wracking challenge. Mostly baron scenery of dry land and mountains through the eastern part of Iran we made progress but slowly. The camper had an engine problem, something to do with the oil rings and it was burning oil with blue smoke from the exhaust. The assumption was that if we took it easy, it would last until we were back in the UK, so we travelled at a modest pace of 50-60 kilometres per hour. Going slower would also save fuel as between us we didn't have money to waste. Someone they had spoken to said that there was a route to the north of Tehran along the coast of the Caspian Sea which was beautiful and picturesque and a pretty good surface. The route would take us through a mountainous area, but of course, if we were on the coast of the sea, it should be fairly flat and passable and more interesting. It was also 100 kilometres shorter in distance. Some people that they had met suggested this as the southern route was desert and sparsely populated without many facilities and a very bumpy road. Their concern was about the campers' suspension, it was bad for about 600 km; we opted for the northern route.

On the first evening, we set off to cross the mountains heading for Bojnurd, after a while it became dark. The road was good for quite some time; then we rose into a mountainous area again which always makes things a bit tricky in the dark. The road narrowed and now winding around and over the mountains and became dangerous. As we rounded a bend, there were huge boulders across the width of the road; we just managed to stop in time before we ran into them. Suddenly three soldiers appeared from nowhere pointing rifles at us and said we should get out of the vehicle. They asked for our papers and began to be rather puzzled as to why we were there. Only one spoke some English, but basically, after telling them we were on our way to Turkey, they asked why we had taken this road. It was very unusual to have five English tourists in the middle of the night in such a remote location; for them, it had never happened before. We told them the story we had heard from people we had met saying that the route was very beautiful and if we had the chance we should take it and see the small villages and the hospitality of the people there. The road also took us through a national park called Golestan which was mountains and forest which were worthwhile seeing. They calmed down from their first guarded approach and were pleased that we were interested in their area, with one soldier roughly translating it turned out that one of them lived in the nearby town. We were close to Bojnurd at the start of the Park so we asked if we could pass. The soldiers said it wasn't illegal to pass but that it was too dangerous to go any further in the dark and if we wished to carry on it wasn't just the quality of the road, there were also bandits, for our safety we should wait until it was light. We thanked them and pulled into some flat ground 100 metres from the roadblock and slept, the soldiers said that they would be there until the morning and they would watch out for us. The bandit problem was a difficult one to deal with mentally. You were either attacked or not. There was nothing in between. If we had been given information about that area from someone having made the trip, they may just have been lucky and had no trouble. It didn't mean that we wouldn't have trouble. The soldiers made us think of that. It just wasn't worth taking the chance and exposing ourselves to the risk, particularly if we had been advised not to.

In the morning they had cleared the boulders from the road, so we were able to carry on. Most of the scenery was stunning maybe some 3000 feet above sea level but up and down over mountains and through gorges and passes. There were many wild animals in the park but much to our disappointment we didn't see a single one. There were Caspian tigers at one stage, all had died off or been killed by poachers some years back, but the forest was full of wild boar and several types of deer. We stopped at lunch time and bought the standard local flatbread and eggs in a village where we were the centre of attraction especially Anne who was blond. The villagers had never seen any English people, and a blond girl was even rarer. She was an attraction where ever we stopped in both Iran and Turkey. There was resentment from most of the women in the vicinity; they made their displeasure rather obvious for the attention given as men stood and stared not believing what they saw having never seen one in the flesh. I must admit it was creepy, for her it was even creepier, but as we were three men, there was no approach from the men. The women were far more menacing.

By the afternoon after another stop for fuel, we had left the park and were heading for Goran. We passed through in the evening time. It is a large city more organised and was far less wild than Afghanistan. After topping up the tank and spare cans we travelled the 30 km or to the coast of the Caspian Sea. After a short while, the road took us away from the coast heading west for Sari where we would then cut north to the coast. We were still fresh and decided to carry on along the coast. It went dark, and within a short distance the road deteriorated, it wasn't long before we encountered another boulder roadblock the same as the last just before the coastal town of Bobalsar. The soldiers came at us again with rifles. Just because it was the second time in a short space of time didn't make it any less frightening. This lot could just as easily have shot us too. Also, these guys were more official and officious and had us out of the camper on the roadside. There was a checkpoint hut type thing into which they took our documents, we waited for what seemed like hours but was maybe 30 minutes. The road from there was supposed to be very picturesque with some small country villages. Although we knew we might have to wait until the morning to pass, we were looking forward to this part of the trek. It was not to be; the soldiers said that we must go south and head for Tehran as it was not possible to pass even in the daytime. It was a sensitive military area and prohibited. Bob tried to argue as he had been told by other travellers that came from the west that there was a passage allowed, how could they have known what it was like if they had not been there? The soldiers were having none of our stories, and we were told to turn around and take another route. There was another road we could take around the roadblock to resume the planned route, but the soldiers had warned us about bandits, they could have been exaggerating, but we decided not to take the chance. We were disappointed but thought it worthless to argue any further. We decided to go back to Sari for the night, as we knew what to expect having just travelled the road and then find a route further south to Tehran in the morning.

As it became light we found another bakery and had breakfast but this time inside what was a café with huge glass windows. Word spread like wildfire and the locals came out in force to see these English people in their town. All the children and some of the adults had their faces flattened against the glass just staring at us. If only they knew how weird and frightening they looked, faces distorted through trying to get closer to see better or something. As we came out, we had twenty or so follow us to the camper. The young boys were noisy and tried to speak to us, but within a short space of time all they could say was Bobby Charlton, Bobby Charlton, and they chanted this until we got inside the camper. I'm sure they were just fascinated to see us, but it was rather menacing as there were so many of them each pushing to get closer and chanting even louder. Now we were inside their faces were flattened against the windows of the camper windows, this was even more menacing, an array of flattened crazy smiling faces making loads of noise, we were thankful to be pulling away. The windows were a mess, it was tempting to shout at them to go but we wondered what sort of reaction that would create. We always thought that the slightest thing could make a situation nasty very quickly.

With plenty of fuel, we headed west to the next town and then south over the mountains towards the desert road which went on west to Tehran. As we dropped down the mountains, it was a pleasant 18 degrees or so. As we approached the desert road, it was maybe 25 degrees. Things were going well until we had a flat tyre. It took a while to change and then off again. Within 10 kilometres we had another. This time with no spare and managed to flag down a truck for a lift to the nearest town. Chris and I stayed behind with the girls while Bob went off to find a garage for the repairs. It took ages, but by late afternoon he had the garage owner drop him back to the van. By the time we had finished, we had gone into the town for some food and decided to do the 120 km into Tehran in the morning. The guy with the garage let us park on his land next to his house on the forecourt was a bit of added security.

-oo-

We were away early in the morning about 8 am thinking that we would hit Tehran after the rush hour if there were one. It was just over 100 km so we would be there around 10 am. It was a bright day, Bob was driving and Chris in the front, I was in the back with the two girls. The road was straight and one lane each way but wide. Each side of the road there was a considerable flat area of at least a kilometre of sand with a few rocks backdropped by baron, rocky mountains and hills. Occasionally there were side roads from both sides, and we were some 500mts behind a car in front of us. We were all feeling rested having not overdone the driving in the last couple of days when suddenly a taxi, which had stopped at the junction we approached, as we were passing him pulled straight out in front of us. There wasn't even a second to brake, and we hit the front wing with our near side front (the off side of course as we were driving on the right-hand side of the road), where Chris was sitting. He shouted some expletives as he shot forwards and hit the windscreen at the same time as Bob. The three of us in the back bowled into the back of both of the front seats as we were lazing on the flattened bed we hadn't folded away. The taxi had slewed round and was in facing the oncoming traffic in the middle of their lane. We were all ok, shaken no cuts or bruises or anything broken.

We had the two punctures the day before, so we thought we had already had our fair share of incidents for a while, but it wasn't to be; now we were in a crash in the middle of Iran without a clue as to what we should do next. We knew we were in the right but what difference would that make? Of course, we all piled out of the camper to the taxi driver shouting and gesturing with his hands to say look what you have done to my car. We all spoke at once saying that it wasn't our fault, he was the one that pulled out in front of our path. He didn't speak a word of English, neither did his passenger. Before long there were several people stopped, as we were blocking the road, and gathering around us and the cars in the middle of the road. Then a bus stopped, and all the passengers got out looking and making a comment about what was happening. It was bedlam and very worrying. Anything could have been spoken about and concocted, shifting the blame to us. None of them knew what was happening, of course, they were only guessing, and within minutes it seemed like they all had their version of the crash. Eventually, a guy came up to us who had been behind us, and he said he had seen it all…and spoke enough English to communicate and was saying that it was the taxi drivers fault. Phew! We all breathed a sigh of relief and encircled him as the taxi driver went quiet and went over to his passenger. We were eager to take the details of anyone that had seen it and who was willing to say so. The guy who spoke English calmed everyone down and said that we must now wait for the police.

By this time there were long lines of traffic in both directions and all by this time were in the process of driving onto the sand off the road and round our two vehicles blocking it. The dust was dreadful, and before long another bus came along with two local Gendarmes. These guys were in fatigue type uniforms and boots and unarmed. They were support for the police and just cruised around on public transport helping out with whatever they could where there was trouble. Our situation was one of the exact reasons for their deployment. They marshalled the traffic and asked if we could move the camper and the taxi so that they were not blocking the road. By this time it was quite serious as we were on the main road in and out of the city. We said that as the police had not arrived, that wasn't a good idea, the position of the vehicles told the story of what had happened. They assured us the first witness had explained what he saw and that they could see what had gone on. It was not possible to wait to clear the road for the police to deal with it as they could be hours as they had to come from Tehran and the traffic was piling up for miles. That was a bit worrying as we had no intention of waiting around for hours.

Looking at the damage, although all the front passenger side was crumpled and the headlight and indicator glasses were broken but the bodywork was not badly crushed, the wheel was free and no problem to drive. We agreed to move it to the side of the road. The taxi was also driveable, and this too was taken to the side of the road, there was surprisingly little damage for the magnitude of the crash. The taxi driver after much deliberation with the Gendarmes disappeared an hour or so later. If we could not leave, why is the other driver and vehicle involved in the accident, particularly the one who was in the wrong, allowed to go? It all seemed a bit one-sided, nobody spoke English of any worth, except the witness, communication was through gestures. There was only slight damage to our vehicle we suggested we should leave and we were not bothered by any compensation damage. Just communicating this idea took some time. Each time they didn't understand what we were trying to say, they became more annoyed at us being persistent and them not understanding. A further deep concern came over all of us as by this time there were 4 Gendarmes, another two had stepped off a bus to join the first two. Several conversations went on between them and a witness of the incident which was now some two hours ago.

Thankfully one of the two new officers spoke a little English, and we were able to put over the idea of us leaving which they said was not possible. We said that we would go to the police station to report the crash and make a statement but that was not possible either. There was still a suspicion that we could be in trouble as on top of the worry that we were pretty much the foreign outsiders, anything could have been said and agreed between them and by now they had let the only English speaking witness go. There seemed something that we were not aware of, some higher order of what had happened we were more enquiring of the officer that had some English but then he closed down. Something didn't add up. Six hours after the crash we were sitting, half in and out of the camper and in and out of the hot sun. There was no shade except for inside the camper that was now stifling. Other people in civilian clothes had joined the Gendarmes who appeared seemed to know each other. Shortly after the officer who spoke English flagged down a bus and disappeared. Between us, we gathered up the kit we had taken out of the van and Bob slid across the seats and jumped into the driving seat. We had decided to make a run for it. They didn't have any radios so it would take some time until someone had gone into Tehran or connected to someone else that could report us. We thought we could be miles away by then. Anne had left a pair of shoes outside of the van so that it would not be too obvious that we were going. Bob started the engine hurriedly shoved it into gear, we all piled in through the side door and slammed it shut leaving the decoy shoes behind. The Gendarmes went crazy, running down the road after us and screaming what must have been 'stop', but we had got away.

It wasn't long, only a minute or so that it started to dawn on us that we were still some way outside of Tehran and the only way past it was through it. The biggest city for miles around and it was where the police station was. A strange new place would take some navigating and take whatever time, and we would stand out like a sore thumb in an English registered vehicle, the only English vehicle for hundreds of miles and one involved in a crash where the police were aware. We had not thought it through properly, all this tumbled into our minds now within two or three kilometres away from the crash site. We stopped on the side of the road and decided quickly it best to go back and straight away. If we left it any longer, we wouldn't have much of a defence if they had caught us and taken us back, or even worse to the police station and jail!

We turned around and drove back. By this time we passed a bus which one of the officers we had left behind had already caught and was already on his way to report the now new incident at the police station we guessed. He saw us and stopped the bus, and he walked back returning some minutes later. As we arrived, the two remaining officers were understandably anxious. All we could do was try through gesture to explain that we had thought better of escaping and of course we had left a pair of shoes. We also handed them the keys to assure them we were not going to try the same trick again. They relaxed a little, it was the first sign that they appeared human and any of them had shown some empathy for us and our situation, but not that much. Shortly after, the officer that had left earlier before we had made a break for it returned and brought a bag full of kebabs and salad. We said that we were worried when he left; he was the only person with whom we could communicate. We were also very insecure and still felt that there was some ulterior and serious element to our predicament which they were not telling us which intensified our need to get away. We kept asking why they had let the taxi driver go and why not us.

We were thankful for the food. It was now late afternoon. We had been there from breakfast time, some eight or nine hours earlier that day. The officers were restless too. Although it must have been an easy day for them without too much serious trouble to sort out they were bored, we all were. It was somewhat of a gathering place by now. A few locals had stopped, and again some of them appeared to know one or the other of the Gendarmes. At one stage there must have been ten or eleven people milling around, some just being nosey or curious pouring over probably the biggest event in the district for years. It must have been quite a spectacle to see five English people in an English car having crashed into a local taxi. You could see them looking around at the tyre marks and broken glass making comments to the officers appearing to be knowledgeable about these things.

Eventually, about 7.30 or 8.00 pm two four-wheel drive police cars arrived much to our relief. They spoke to the officers we had spent the day with but didn't say a word to us. When we tried to speak to them, they turned away and ignored us. The tension now was even greater. From the first sigh of relief at the sight of a real policeman's uniform, to be blanked again was a worry. What had gone on for the whole of the day? What had they said about our situation? There was disdain from them, and the Gendarmes who had at one stage started to be a bit more communicative, they too went cold with us. Another police car pulled into the side of the road. The situation was overwhelming. A slight crash that wasn't our fault where we were not concerned about compensation for the damage, a string of officers, onlookers and locals totalling maybe fifteen people, two police cars and then a third turned up with three people inside, all twelve hours after the incident. Surely it was not a normal situation, all of them talking to each other and not us, over a small interaction at a junction in the middle of the desert outside of the capital city of Iran. What on earth was happening?

The latest car drew to a stop. There were three people in this one to add to the throng, a driver and passenger and someone in the back. We were reeling, all day and the best part of twelve hours in the hot, dusty desert air and under stress at having been held for so long. The worst bit was that there were no updates as to why it was taking so long, what possible reason could there be

146

to be made to wait the whole day? Now, after all this time, where we imagined some semblance of authority would deal with our predicament we had the disappointment that no one was speaking to us at all or asking questions about the incident, almost as if we were not there. As if it was all done and dusted, we were the ones at fault, and we were going to spend years in an Iranian prison. Albeit in slight gest, Chris and I looked at each other and, thinking that we had won the pools in hitching a lift back to England, maybe it would have been better for us to struggle and go to the British embassy to ask if they would repatriate us. Maybe now we would be seeing the British consul sooner than we thought in the different light of being banged up in jail in Tehran. Although in jest, it was a very real and horrifying thought.

The passenger side door of the rather more upmarket gleaming police sedan flung open, and a young officer quickly went to open the back door where another policeman appeared. This officer was a whole lot different; not dressed in fatigues or civils, this was Mr Ego himself! Immaculately dressed in uniform with his jacket resting on his shoulders without his arms in the sleeves, still wearing sunglasses even though it was almost dark, there appeared what could only be the chief of the police station in Tehran, neigh, the police chief of the whole of Iran.

Pristine and smelling of expensive aftershave speaking in perfect English, "I like the English" were the first words he uttered. He took one look at the crowd and screamed some order that everyone heard. The locals disappeared in a split second, the Gendarmes quickly climbed into the other police cars and waited for the next instruction. He introduced himself as Colonel Hassan Madani and profusely but with a stern reserve apologised for the delay. We, of course, all nervously spoke at once grateful that finally, we had met someone who could understand not only the words but the subtleties of what had happened communicated in English of course, with a vague notion that it would be understood. He closed us all down saying that he knew we had crashed earlier, he was still investigating the incident. There had been much fuss because we had committed a serious crime in trying to escape the scene of an accident. It started to dawn on us again how quickly things can go wrong. Throughout the time we had been waiting we had in our heads mitigated our attempt to escape by our returning and handing the keys over so that there was no opportunity to repeat it. Right now a little scared, we were glad we had. Even though it had taken them so long to get there, surely it can't be such a serious crime?

But that wasn't where the police chief started his thinking. All speaking at once again we tried to mitigate our case by trying to explain all that had happened. He said there would be plenty of time for all that when we arrived at the police station. Our hearts and faces sunk into despair, it all sounded very much like we would all be arrested. He did, however, restate the point of saying that he liked English people and that he spoke English well because his parents had sent him to university in the UK. He was full of himself, there was no wonder that the conversation was all about him. At least this comment gave a glimmer of hope that there may be an element of discussion before we were dragged screaming into Iranian prison cells. His eye caught a glimpse of the two girls, "These two can come with me in my car," and signalled the plan was that the rest of us to go in the camper with the policeman that was the passenger in the chief's car. The girls said no, quite understandably they did not want to do that because they were afraid to be on their own even with the policemen. The chief was offended but suddenly realised their fear and allowed one of the girls into the camper and Chris travelled with the other in the police car. The cavalcade of cars like a maximum security serious criminal transfer with the two Jeeps in front of us and the chief behind with sirens blasting, set off and sped along the road and suburbs of Tehran through into the city centre. All the vehicles arrived at the police station at the same time and as we neared the station, they obviously heard the sirens, the noise now was deafening in the narrow side street. The gates opened and we went inside the car parking area. Even that was worrying; we felt like it was the route for hardened criminals with the least chance of any escape as after entering, the gates were closed behind us by two guards. It was a dimly lit parking area, the corridors inside were even dimmer but at least Chris, the two girls and I were again together. Bob had been asked to take his documents to have them registered through at the front of the station, so the Colonel informed us.

Still wired with the myriad of possibilities of what could happen next and after being whisked up out of the desert, after a brief wait in the yard we were guided into the office of the chief. He was already hanging his jacket on a coat hanger on a stand, now showing the whole of his immaculately pressed shirt, along with his scramble egg braided hat on a hook above. By this time he had taken off the sunglasses, and he was bristling, back in his territory now and proud of every single inch of its floor space and every stick of expensive, traditional polished hardwood furniture. In came trays of tea and coffee. "This is my office, and only I have the qualifications to question you properly as I have good English. It will save a lot of misunderstandings that may arise from you talking my officers that don't have my command of your language." That was sensible we all thought, the relief was plain to see in all our faces as we looked approvingly across at each other and back to him. "I have brought you here so you can see and I want you to relax and take time to explain to me why you tried to escape," he said in a very imposing no-nonsense official tone. The way he said it smacked of 'brought you here instead of the cells or interrogation rooms', scary!

He was skilled in dealing from the top to get the answers to his questions and used to trying to put people at a disadvantage. "It does not look very good for you to do this, my officers said that they treated you well and brought you food and it was a shock to them for you to try to get away in such a desperate fashion." The Gendarmes had put the story across that they were being sociable and had brought us the food, but that wasn't until after the escape attempt we explained. He knew what had happened, as quick as a flash in an experienced retort he said, "Yes but they went for it before you tried to abscond." It became clear that much of the incident was spoken about in Tehran throughout the day. Some of the people who had come to the scene and left must have been from the station gathering information and reported back.

It took a while for us to establish that they had not told us they were going for food, let alone that there would be food for us. Up until that time, everyone appeared hostile to us. The Gendarmes let the taxi driver go and yet had us wait for twelve hours for his good self to arrive. Why did they not let us go too? Or why did they not keep the taxi driver too? After all, he was the other party in the accident, was this not favouring the local person with special attention above mere foreigners? "No, not at all, I had heard that you were there, and of your circumstances. I have told you I liked the English; I was looking forward to meeting with you."

"You put my officers in a very difficult position; they thought they could trust you." We made sure that he realised that we were far from being aware of anything. All we knew was the hostility of being held in the desert in the middle of nowhere in the blazing heat through the whole day for something that wasn't our fault and where the other party to the crash had been set free. He listened in silence.

All five of us contributed to the response and confirmed the facts. Colonel Hassan Madani was good at his job, but by this stage, he was thoroughly enjoying the questioning and particularly as he had the opportunity to practice his English. He then started to play a little and sport with us. Reading between the lines, as the conversation unfolded, it appeared that the officers had to take a reprimand for allowing us to get away. He was trying to apportion some blame to us in defence of them. More and more it became obvious that we had caused trouble for them and alarm in the station at just why we had attempted. He started to give a more humorous account saying that everyone there mocked the Gendarmes for not being able to control five unknown English tourists never mind drug dealers or terrorists. It had caused such a stir.

Further, we explained our experiences in Afghanistan and how bad they had been with us merely over an alarm clock. Immediately after the crash, the taxi driver was hostile in a similar way. We didn't know what to expect and thought the worst. There seemed to be something more to the encounter with the taxi driver. He was so aggressive with us and yet it was blatantly his fault. Anyway, we came back and gave the keys. Surely this was an admission of our wrongdoing and trying to put it right. Why were we the only ones held? In mitigation, in the UK, we would never wait so long just for the police to come to a minor accident with no one injured. With a wry smile, Chris by now feeling more at ease and a little frisky. From much experience of him, this usually means it could be trouble. But deftly he says, "Come on Colonel, you are an intelligent man and have some experience of police procedures in the UK, you must understand our straight British mentality, there was no malice in the actions we took, we were just fearful in a strange place." In a kind of a compliment and Mickey take adds, "You also dress very well and take care of your appearance; surely, it wasn't merely the time taken in preparation for your day's work that left us with twelve hours to wait for you." We were doing so well up to then. Bob, who had come back from the paper session recoiled in horror into the corner, the two girls spluttered trying to keep back a belly laugh, terrified that the Colonel's ego would kick in and he would take it the wrong way. I threw my head back and stiffened up waiting for him to grab the phone and make a call for someone to burst in with five pairs of handcuffs. He and we all laughed eventually but only after what seemed to be a long pause (the pause, albeit at first a nervous one, did heighten the amusement) as the Colonel was still trying to keep his composure, the comment from Chris sent us close to the brink of it all going wrong. As it turned out, we were missing a chunk of the story governing the circumstances and attitudes.

All of this constructive and humorous banter and finally Chris's cheek did catch him out, and we could see that he had something more and he was waiting to tell us. By now he could see that we were somewhere up there, we were a match for his intellect and we could see that he was beside himself. There was something that had made the situation seem so out of proportion. He quickly called for some more tea and said, "I must confess, there are special circumstances regarding the taxi driver which may have made it difficult for you to understand. They may all have appeared to have treated you differently, but not because you were foreigners and the taxi driver a local. I was not sure whether I should tell you but trust that it will not be a problem as you will soon be gone." Up to that point we were filled with anticipation and dread of what was going to happen to us and that was his first firm indication that we were going to be set free and some of the terror of being jailed lifted. Phew, we wouldn't be asking the embassy to come and try to bail us out as criminals. "One reason for the delay in reaching you today was that we made several arrests of a drug-dealing ring. As part of the sting to catch them, an undercover detective was posing as a taxi driver listening for conversations of drug traffickers and he was the one you collided with."

"It was very embarrassing for this to happen to him and for it to involve much wanted foreign tourists in my country." The clever Colonel had saved the best bit until last, and it was indeed, ironic, and he amusing. We twelve hours in the hot sun and here sat on the edge of our seats for more than an hour. It left everyone in the police station wondering what they would do with us and thank goodness for the Colonel's refined background. He had strung us out all the way along with his serious attitude and fastidiousness but showed his character. All in all, he was a very good man. So, ridiculous as it may seem, all the strange attitudes and misunderstandings had been because we had inadvertently and unwittingly been involved in a Tehran drug bust. All the Gendarmes and detectives etc., especially after letting us escape, were fearful of their jobs if they did anything else wrong. It must have been like a Brian Rix farce in and around the station all day. Unbelievable! We had to be there on that day, at that junction and crash with that undercover cop. What on earth would we get involved with next?!

Bob, still recovering from the cheeky quip from Chris and the new revelations, nervously rounded off, "Well that explains a lot of the background perfectly that caused the way in which the Gendarmes treated the taxi driver different than us and the way they spoke to us. It was all for rather different reasons, one of these being their embarrassment, that which we imagined and in turn raising fears of all kinds. Nothing seemed quite to add up, but now it was clear to see. It was also a good explanation for the crash too as, the taxi driver as an undercover cop, he was listening…but not looking!"

The Colonel was please that his presentation of the facts had smoothed over our indignation, in part by deftly putting us on our back foot by maintaining that we were the criminals, wriggling out of the catalogue of the errors and sheer buffoonery his men had gone through as the day unfolded. I can't help thinking that he also manoeuvred the day, irrespective of the inconvenience of us frying in the heat and worrying for twelve hours, purely and simply so that he made some time to clear things up after the drug dealers' arrests. He was saving us until last just to talk to the English for practice. I wouldn't have put it past him. That we played him at his game, worrying as it was, he

152

took in his stride. What a character, the world needs more of
them.

Chapter 11
Multigrade and Kebabs

In analysis through nervous relief, we all felt very pleased with ourselves about the way we all backed each other up and our explanations. It's strange in such alien circumstances you lull yourself into a false sense of insecurity. You're innocent but you think you have got away with something, even if you have done nothing wrong. I'm sure that part of the way it unfolded was the Colonel and his willingness just to talk and have his bit of fun. We said our goodbyes to him and he reluctantly went home after his long day. Bob went into the police garage, they even did their repairs to the police cars on the premises, to talk to the engineers about the damage now that the full story had come out and they admitted it was the policeman's fault. They said if we waited for a couple of days they would make the repairs. We explained that we were in a bit of a hurry to get back to the UK, there were still several thousands of kilometres to go and we wanted to be on our way. They ended up giving some $20 for the replacement parts as the work there would cost thee nothing done in the garage. If we had have waited, they would have done it for us. They fitted new lamps in the headlight and indicators so that they would work and used tape to cover the broken lenses. We were just happy that we were not in any more serious trouble. The police chief was happy because it cost virtually nothing for them and…we were on our way again.

It was a long, gruelling drive ahead of us from there to Istanbul, our next significant aiming point as the crossover to Europe. We had travelled by hook or by crook all the way from Australia with all but the week on the cruise ship on Asian territory. By this stage, we were quietly looking forward to seeing some surroundings that were less alien to us. We were not wishing the time and travelling away, but with the journey plan pretty much cut and dried through unbelievably good fortune, somehow we now had the feeling of missing a more familiar environment. Up until about then we had not spent a lot of time thinking about being back. There just wasn't the time in the day to stop and lull ourselves into that security we knew. Nor did we want to, but Iranian crashes, absconding from the scene of an accident and Tehran drug busts aside, the more relaxed sitting and driving in the camper allowed us a bit more head space. It was very new to imagine that we only had the one vision of how we should get back to the UK to contemplate. Up until then, it was always a multiple choice decision to make as to how and which way we would go with a barrow of awkward and complicated governing factors. It made the UK seem that much nearer although it certainly wasn't, there was still many miles to go. We had made a historical connection in the Colonel, the stuff of great memories; I am sure that had he not been involved in the incident with his character, things could have turned out very badly for us all. It was a good example of the value of having someone sympathetic to us in otherwise pretty hostile surroundings.

Before we left him we spent time explaining what we had done before we met the others and what we planned to do to complete the journey. More tea, coffee and sweets appeared at intervals. Our trip was all before the Ayatollah in the more romantic time when it was still really Persia ruled by the Shah. The Colonel was straight from that time of Eastern autocratic rule by a sovereign and not by a fundamental Islamic cleric. More of an accent on dressing up rather than blowing up. Although not getting caught up in the politics, to us then it seemed much more friendly and palatable than it does now. The Colonel, I am sure he had his unfathomably barbarous moments, westernised through his education. He had many of the attributes and outlooks that we could relate to and did appreciate the British organised way of life and that, even with its British flaws, it had the history of perfecting an organised society. He could appreciate the irony we saw and the discomfort we suffered in having to wait for twelve hours for the police service to sort out our incident of very small proportions. The others around us didn't seem to have that concept; they just accepted that it was the way things happened there and couldn't see why we were put out in any way. We thought it was ridiculous and yet, they thought it was normal. The very basis of misunderstanding that could lead to any number of bad results.

The main thing, as in other the many other situations that we had encountered, was to maintain a good attitude. It was just something we did without at the time having the conscious notion that the cause of most misunderstandings is, ten per cent though disagreement and a lofty ninety per cent through attitude while in the disagreement. As with other examples of our behaviour, it just came out, we must have had a reasonable upbringing somewhere along the line. Of course, we didn't always maintain a good attitude, but it was part of what we were trying to exercise on the trip at the same time as learning about others' ways of life. We saw it work time after time and we saw what happened if we were not so patient. The Afghan border problem was a sparkling example of how not to do things.

--oo--

We hadn't expected to spend the whole day just waiting outside of Tehran, it all worked out ok finally apart from the delay but it was a heck of an example of how rapidly things can go off track. But, hellfire, we were from Poulton and by now pretty experienced travellers. We could deal with anything that confronted us, as we had done to date with more than the average amount of luck. People say that you make your own luck, if so we were just good at it, without thinking. By this time it was very late at night when we finally got away. We decided to find our way out of the city and find somewhere on the outskirts, not too remote and sleep until it was light before we started the trip. At first light, we were gone after filling the tank and heading north.

At last, we were cruising, taking stock and chatting with Bob and the two girls of the experiences of before we met them and of places they had not been. They were listening while we had the Colonel captivated with the story of the Chinese guy, Charlie in Malaya and one story led to another as they were asking questions to fill in the gaps caused by all the worries cluttering our brains in his office. They were fascinated by the press cards and university ID cards, the quality and the discounts that were possible, just as we still were.

We still had around 2500 kilometres to go to get to Istanbul. It was a long way at 60 kph, the engine was not sounding good and in perfect health and better we took it easy. An extra day or two would be infinitely better than breaking down which may take an extra week or two, Notwithstanding the cost of any trouble which Chris and I had no way of making any contribution to fixing. There was a certain amount of apprehension. Since we met them and set off we had already been confronted twice with armed guards, been diverted a gunpoint, had two punctures (could have happened to anyone anywhere), a crash and the best part of arrested involving a drugs bust. Pretty good going for the first few days! All this when on meeting at the border post of Herat back in Afghanistan, we had no idea that any of these things happen, not a clue. The fact was, you couldn't have made it up! Now we had a bit more time to contemplate the past events and what was happening. With these things in mind, interspersed with tides of laughter we couldn't help but wonder what on earth could happen next. Don't forget that they also had the backdrop of one of their numbers being held hostage so we knew that there was nothing outside of the possible.

Bob did most of the driving, it was his choice, he must have felt more secure. After all, he had experience of driving the camper on the outward journey and it was his vehicle in the UK, we were not but we did drive some of the stages. He was also taking the time not to be so involved with us and particularly Anne and sorting his head out with what was happening with their relationship. It couldn't have been easy for him especially as, in such close surroundings and she was giving me attention. It must have been difficult for him. Throughout the whole time, we may only have had one or two moments where he would feel awkward and gave a disapproving look or a curt word. He did manage very well; I was impressed but never looked any deeper into it, it wasn't my problem. We were on our way to Tabriz and north not far from the Armenian border to the border towns of Buzagan, on the Iranian side and Gurbulak in Turkey. We had decided on the northern route which was shorter by about 300 kilometres through their outward journey experience of the more southern route which had uneven road surfaces. It was like continually running over ripples in the road surface. Although the south road took you through Ankara, which the northern route didn't to our disappointment, the north was a better road and a cooler temperature which was wise for the sake of the air-cooled engine that was feeling the strain. Good thinking from Bob at the time.

I'm sure the roads there now are much better in comparison to now, at the time there was much to take into consideration as to the condition when deciding a suitable route. In the UK you decide on where you are going and pick the most suitable depending on what you want. The scenery of inland or coastal, the speed you wish to achieve whether it's via motorways or smaller roads or certain places etc. At that time in such places, there were a host of other considerations. Gathering information about the conditions, whether anyone had travelled that route in the past and any intrinsic dangers of the conditions, severe weather, attacks by bandits or local police or military or other corrupt officials accepted practices of collecting cash for themselves. A myriad of things to take into consideration above what you would traditionally expect to take into account back in Britain.

That's why the Colonel in Tehran was so valuable. He wanted to show that he ran a ship that did not tolerate such things (in all probability corruption was writhe anyway), he took pride in demonstrating this, thank goodness for our sakes. But for him being the way he was with us and trying to impress, I am sure that as a minimum, it would have cost money to get the camper back and longer to get back on our way. Who would we tell of corruption? Report them to the Embassy? What would or could the consulate do to help? If we had created a fuss, somewhere literally down the road later in the same country there would be trouble waiting. Another arrest for something ridiculous, and there would be nothing you could do to stop it. It's not until something unjust happens, that you realise it actually can and does happen. Just like the boyfriend of Christine and the alarm clock in Herat. Without some influence or a lot of luck, there is nothing you can do. It's far more sensible just to pay your way out of a situation. Yes it still goes on now, I'm sure to a degree in the UK too but the degree and openness in these places, particularly back in those times, was hard to comprehend. Nowadays they have police to watch the police and it is more covert as they have to be seen to be doing the right things but it continues today in large portions.

We travelled to Tabriz in total some 630 kilometres and decided to stop there the night. Parked up in a large car park we spoke to the local police about travelling to the north and they advised against us going that route from anywhere past Erzincan. It was related to some stretches of road damaged from some trouble with security forces and weather etc. which left us to contemplate the southern route. At least Bob and the others had experience of it leaving less room for us to go astray knowing the critical points of direction changes etc. But there was a road just after Erzincan, that took us a bit south and through Ankara. Fuelled and fed we were away early in the morning heading north for almost 200 kilometres from Tabriz to Bazargan on the Iranian side and cross the border into Turkey at Gurbulak. We arrived at about 11 am, it was sunny and about 12 degrees, noticeably colder as we were now further north. It is the most major border point between the two countries for import and export. The customs were quite fastidious with their inspection of the camper and our luggage. With the van up on a lift, two customs officials with lights and screwdrivers examined and poked around for some time. After the all clear the van was brought back down for the inside to be inspected, all clear there too. They emptied out all our luggage on tables in a shed and were most put out not to find anything we should not have had. Not only were they looking for drugs and guns but they were as interested to see if we had any pornographic material. Never even occurred to us that would be on their list.

Although the whole experience took 3 hours, we wandered over and climbed into the van, again thinking we had got away with something. We hadn't really; it was just a relief because we got away from them and didn't have any trouble, all crazy but true. By now we had started subconsciously to build a healthy appreciation of things not going wrong. They seemed convinced that they would find something, thank goodness they didn't. Now it was a trek through some desert and what looked to be more mountains for the next 500 kilometres and around 1550 kilometres to Istanbul to which none of us was looking forward. We had started to develop a greater sense of 'getting there' by now, rather than an interest in the places where we were travelling through, without actually thinking about it. At our speed, this leg was the best part of three days driving. It was 300 kilometres to Erzurum and a further 200 kilometres to Erzincan. That would see us to the end of the day and we could overnight there and decide what was next ready for the morning. If the road to the north was still considered to be a problem, we could turn left at Altkoy about another 100 kilometres further and carry on through Ankara. All sounds good as a plan, of course we had no idea of the roads or what we would encounter but you have to start with some idea of where you were going.

We talked to pass the time. The countryside was much the same from then on and slow going. As we were focussing on just the getting there rather than what was happening around us apart from navigating safely, our outlook was leaning more toward it being a task to do rather than an experience. The road seemed to go on and on with very little difference. It might have been boring but we were still fairly buoyant about the surety of getting back to the UK. Hopefully, we would make it without any foreseen obstacles. After all, what could go wrong now? Silly question as we all said to one another. Just look what had happened in the last few days. We didn't see that lot beforehand. Who on earth could have imagined it? The 300 kilometres to Erzurum went slowly and we arrived at about 7.30 pm, picked up some food on the west side of the city and found a place to park and sleep. It was very welcome, no one had a lot to say and it seemed like by the time we had nodded off, it was coming light again. Eggs and bread for breakfast, some more fuel and we were off again. We would catch up on the state of roads when we arrived in Erzincan which was the last major city before the turning south if we had to. It was considerably colder now and it may be a better choice to keep to the south. The northern route if open would save some 100 kilometres. As we arrived in Erzincan we found the police station. They said the northern route was bad, thwarted with security problems, for whatever reason. The weather now had closed in and it would not be wise to go there at all and certainly not their recommendation. That was enough convincing. Even though the route was shorter, sliding around on snow and ice may mean we wouldn't get back at all, never mind just delayed waiting for snow ploughs or the like. We opted for going south and through Ankara. It was now noon and we decided to make tracks and have food later. We drove until we wanted to sleep and stopped in a village still about 700 kilometres away from Istanbul.

Making an early start we had a good day's driving, by the evening we were approaching Istanbul. The camper engine was now making more noise than before and burning oil and giving less power. It didn't sound good at all but was still going and if we took it steady, should get us back to England. We thought it better to stay outside of the busy metropolis that night and carry on through during the day. The next day we were in the city and the engine was about to stop. It was clattering and banging with thick smoke coming from the exhaust. All of us on the edge of our seats anxious and disappointed with the prospect, we managed to find a garage only to find that it needed a complete strip down and replacement pistons etc. It had been the subject of a lot of conversation over the last week. It was a major problem especially as Anne had been saying for the last few days that she didn't have enough cash left to repair it. We were hoping that it would last out at least to Europe where we would have more confidence in the mechanics doing a proper job and not charging piles more money because we were foreign and in trouble a long way from home. It wasn't to be, the worst had just happened!

We were in despair, the girls and particularly Christine tearful. All of us had been building up to the ferry ride across the Channel after the last leg in Europe to France and then seeing the white cliffs of the UK. Our dream was shattered. Chris and I began to draw up contingency plans. It would be difficult but we could fall back on the repatriation idea, if they would do it. Organising money from the UK for the flights back was another option, we could try to hitch a lift again was the third. Bob said he would bet that Anne had the money to do the work as she was always squirrelling money away somewhere, but she hadn't. The decision was made for them to have a friend from the UK transfer some money. She went into a bank after phone calls and organised for it. What a relief, it would take a little more time but at least there was no need for the contingency plan any more.

While Anne was fixing the transfer, we would see if we could get a better price from another garage. It turned out that, provided there were no other problems with the engine, the first garage had given the best price so we went back. It would take three days to find the parts and do the work and we said we would have the work done provided that we could sleep in the camper, in the garage. We hardly had the money for the repairs and certainly didn't have money for hotels. They were very reluctant but finally agreed as long as they could lock the place up when they left and we could not go out until the following morning. Also, once the workers and boss had gone, we couldn't step out of the camper. At night they had a guard dog that wandered round free and it was too dangerous to be on the workshop floor. So we slept for two nights in the camper in the garage on stands unable to even go to the toilet after they were gone. We did this each day, each morning going out sightseeing around the old city near the Blue Mosque and along the river. At the end of the second day, they said it would be ready the next morning. As we had all got to know each other the mechanics and the boss, they thought it was amusing us staying in the camper in the garage, that evening brought us food and we all ate together. They knew we didn't have much money so it was thoughtful of them. After we were so sceptical of them, they were offended and had decided to help us change our minds. They did, they were charming and bought some wine to boot.

The next morning there was some other problem with the engine and it required another part which they didn't have. It took until later in the afternoon to find. We were hoping to be out of the city in the daylight but it was dark by the time it was fixed and we had made our way to the ferry to cross the Bosporus. The ferries, there was no major bridges then, were fascinating. They ran across the river driven by a wheel connected to a chain in the river. It was busy in the city and there were large queues to cross. Hustled into a small space on this rusty antiquated ship we felt out of place without another English car or people near or anywhere around. It felt unfriendly and dangerous so dangerous we had to stay in the camper for the trip unable to take in the sight of crossing the Bosphourous. In fact, with all the noise and frenzy it was difficult just to orientate yourself and identify anything around. There was somehow a bit of security in the fact that we didn't have to engage with anyone. Soon we would be in Europe and the ancient city of Constantinople and boundary with the East would be crossed and left behind. It was a target in our minds all through the trip but more so the nearer we got. With much anticipation, the ferry banged into the other shore and we drove off to complete the last few kilometres of Turkey into to Bulgaria with Yugoslavia, as it was known then next. We had to be gentle with the engine as it was being 'run in' but what the heck. We were on the last leg of an epic trip. While away in Australia we had not missed the UK so much or been home sick or the like but now we were looking forward to being back.

Chapter 12
The New England

The drive into Bulgaria and then through Yugoslavia, that was its name then, was pedestrian in comparison to what we had been through. We stopped for a few hours' sleep outside of Sophia and then carried on. Next up was Austria, Germany, Belgium and then France. Until Sophia, the engine was still 'running in'. As we left, we were now free to go much faster and we made good progress. The focus of emotion in getting back was almost overwhelming. It took over from the sightseeing and wonder of new places. It wasn't that Europe was boring but it was much the same as the UK nothing particularly grabbed our attention. Until then we had been made to concentrate so hard on the task of returning in one piece that it was as if we had been in another world. We had been physically but it was also another world mentally to get the job done, still have fun and experience the difference but with another very serious side to it. It was very demanding, we coped quite well while at the same time maintaining a humanist sense of humour.

Your mental state while having to account for the possibility of someone armed and ready to shoot you, jumping out in front of you has to be conditioned to cope. As a rule, it does not happen in the UK but just imagine it happening, you have not done anything wrong but suddenly you are threatened in this way in an alien culture, anything and everything could go wrong in a breath. Logic is required, which isn't always to hand under duress, somehow you need to maintain the idea that people are fundamentally good and if you demonstrate some good whether it's bearing gifts, showing compassion and empathy or showing you have a sense of humour, whatever, there has to be some giving on your part. If you don't, they don't know that you appreciate that you have it and don't think that you have any right or good in you, because you have not demonstrated it. You have to take the chance. If your point of view is stronger than theirs, you win the situation over and they learn. If theirs is stronger than yours, then they win over the situation and you learn. But whoever wins doesn't matter, so long as it is done for the right reasons. All sound good in theory but not always so easy in practice. There are a host of things that can get in the way of this happening. Your ability to apply critical path thinking to the moment at hand comes into play and any egotistical ideas have got to go and hope you can cope with theirs. This wasn't Buddhism or Zen or any other spiritual teaching, we hadn't studied any of that. As far as we were concerned, it was pure current Poultonian, it was common sense. In a situation of discord, contention or misunderstanding, you have to do something, so until you could fathom what would work, if it hadn't sprung to mind already, the best thing to do was throw in some humour and then see what would work. If we would have bounced off the Colonel's ego, we would have been dead in the water with him. Although he was trying to show us a different side to his culture, he had the power to do whatever he pleased. And probably did for most of his time when there was not someone around that he wished to impress otherwise. This charming man snapped at his officers at the crash site and they moved so quickly you could hardly see them do it. When it does work right and the logic breaks through, as we had demonstrated time after time over the recent weeks, you gain one or the other or both of overwhelming satisfaction or a wealth of learning. That, in part, is what we set out to do while travelling for our own peace and sanity.

The Austrian border was more than halfway to Calais. The overall distance from Istanbul is 3000 kilometres. Here we stopped again for a rest until it was light and carried on. Austria was a place that always interested me from being at school. Up high there was still snow enhancing the sights of houses on the mountainsides and rivers through snow covered fields. I started noticing that all cars were presentable and all looked almost new in comparison with what we had been used to for many weeks of battered wrecks. Things were generally in order and in their place which was noticeable. Everything was relatively clean and people wore clothes that you could relate to have hanging in your wardrobe. Without having been where we were and without having the experience of different things these observations wouldn't have occurred. We were back in our old environment but looking at it in a different light. It started to feel comfortable again but now we were not taking it for granted as we did in the past. We were not thinking to ourselves, yes, yes, we know all about this or that or the other. It was more like, "I know that, isn't it clever or shaped better or ideal," or whatever. Rediscovering what we already knew and taken for granted was a very fulfilling exercise that we were enjoying.

Coming down to the way of the West takes some reconditioning. It was only now that this concept was dawning on both of us. It wasn't that we had become more foreign and their ways were rubbing off on us, it was our minds coping with how they were, we saw it now not having to account for such severe things in different cultures. This process made us recount all the out of normal Western things that happened and the thought patterns that were required to deal with the events and mindsets of those people where we were. You just couldn't look at the local petrol pump attendant in the same way as we did with the armed militia. Back a few thousand kilometres, we hadn't been made Ferrell but we had to cope with those that could be considered as such, certainly about our home experience, education and social construction. It was an odd concept to deal with in the East and certainly sharpened our skill set in contemplating different ways in which people think. It was a constant mental exercise to see and hear and be part of thinking alien to ours. It was Aristotle that once said, although not to us of course, 'a measure of a man's intelligence is being able to consider a concept and not necessarily adopt it'. That's what was apparent as we tuned back into literally not having to deal with constant vast differences of thought and acceptance of their social behaviour. We were going through this process now, albeit that it left us vacant for periods, which wasn't good if driving. Now that we're out of those surroundings, we were 'coming down' to a place of not having to take all those thought processes into account.

Things were different, or back to an accepted norm as in the West. The other effect was, things that you never took a second look at pre the trip, you start seeing as normal. Passing rivers, lakes and canals, the boats were different, back to normal. Houses were different, back to normal. Street signs were different, an alphabet you could read, back to normal. Shops were brightly painted with clean windows with no weird things hanging outside, back to normal. You started relearning appearances of everyday things that pre the trip you never took a second look at. The difference now was that we had seen it, we had seen the vastly different appearances of other cultures and massively different ways of going about everyday things. It was fulfilling and absorbing seeing all these different things but no more fulfilling or absorbing than now being back in the west and appreciating what we had built up surrounding us and the way things are done here. In seeing the richness of other cultures, it was making us appreciate our own more, markedly. When you see things and process what's happening, see how it looks or works, subconsciously you compare how you have seen it appear or work before. When something looks different or doesn't work right, you see the virtue in what was accepted as right initially.

It must be great for born-again Christians (or one of the only benefits of Alzheimer's disease), discovering new things all the time. Our difference was that our vision did not include a man with long hair and a beard, except for William Tell that is, of course, he had a beard and long hair. Chris and I looked at each other and chuckled, our bodies still black and blue through pinching ourselves at our luck. That was enough of that sentimental nonsense for a while. Just suffice to say that we had been through a colossal overseas education, pretty much as overseas as you can get and we now knew a totally different environment that we had survived in and through. Nothing was ever going to be the same again as it was before the trip. We hadn't even got back to the UK and yet we were deep in philosophy. "Didn't even know you were a philosopher," says Chris, "for a moment we were almost serious."

"Must be drunk on the water or the clean Austrian air," I say. Thank goodness we didn't actually see William Tell at the time.

Many people did the same things that we had done along a similar route. At different periods of time, different circumstances prevail. The world is a different place now in comparison. There were no computers, no mobile phones, no Internet and generally no telecommunications as we now know them. There have been several wars in these regions where life and regimes have been changed and then changed again, and then again. A war that starts, and finishes generally bring the infrastructure up to date. As in Afghanistan, most of the conditions that prevailed at the time of our transit are gone forever. Some changes for good and some not so. Even for me now it is hard to imagine how we did it, how we managed without the bags of toys and devices we have at our disposal now, but we managed. Without all these things we still communicated, brought out the best in some people and they did the same with us. Without social media, we communicated with people who responded likewise mainly without judgement and agenda other than getting to know people. Not being angels all the time, we also delved the depths of the opposite things but whatever we did and however we did it, there was no better time spent than when we didn't take things or ourselves too seriously no matter how serious our circumstances were. We thought there just wasn't the time, we were having fun. When we added a bit of humour, even when we were in trouble or about to face some, a way over it, round it or through it emerged and a solution found. We didn't necessarily have the constructed thought in steps that formulated the solution, in the majority of cases, just our attitude provided one. Having that presence of mind was an absolute credit to our upbringing.

Across the border into Germany, we were on the Autobahn and heading for Calais. By 50 kilometres before Frankfurt, we were all tired and Chris said he was ok so he would drive. We said all he had to do was stay on the Autobahn and follow the signs to Brussels. He had 600 kilometres where all he had to do was stay on the motorway. It was around 7 pm in the evening, it was dark and raining, feeling quite confident that nothing could go wrong, after all, we were less than ten hours away from the ferry, we left Chris at the wheel and all slept thinking that by the time we woke we would almost be there. An hour or so later I woke sensing that we were going over a bumpy road and turning corners. This could not be possible, we should be on the motorway, straight for hundreds of kilometres, it couldn't be easier. I clambered to the front seat to find Chris merrily trundling along a country lane, where? I and he had no idea.

168

"Where are we, Chris?" By this time Bob had also woken. "I thought we said just stay on the motorway," says Bob.

"I know what I am doing," he snaps and I curse his father for producing such a bonehead.

"But we are not on the motorway, it's simple, all the way to Brussels and even then on to Calais, there is no need to be anywhere else!" Bob says, astounded. "Look it's just up here, it will only take a minute."

"What's just up here and it will only take a minute to do what?"

I say. Bob turns to me and says, "How the hell did you two manage to get to Afghanistan on your own with him? We left him alone for half an hour, he only had to stay on one road, the biggest road in Germany, where the hell are we now?"

Chris is still adamant he knows what he is doing, "I know where the motorway is."

"Why are we not on it, you shouldn't have to know where it is? You should be on it. How did you get off it?" we replied. He was now in one of those moods where no matter what, he is right, he just didn't get that he had done something wrong by not staying on the one road. I thought thank goodness it's happening, someone else was experiencing what I had to put up with for thousands of kilometres on the way to and the way back from Australia. I had told them about it but they just laughed thinking that we were pulling their legs again but here was the living proof of how Chris could get things catastrophically wrong and frustratingly never admit it. If he did admit it, he would own up to relying on others to get where he wanted to go. If we had not woken, we would probably still be somewhere in Germany, corpses in the camper in some remote area where no one goes and one of life's mysteries as to where on earth we were. Why, how and where he went wrong is still a mystery today. After some forty minutes we re-joined the motorway with Chris saying, "I told you I knew what I was doing, here we are on the motorway." Of course he knew he was wrong, as always, he just couldn't admit it, clown!

Bob took over the driving, this little event had us all awake and realised that, but for a laugh, you couldn't rely on any sense of direction from Chris. We arrived at Calais in the small hour of the morning and took tickets to sail at 9 am, still puzzled as to how he had managed to leave the Autobahn but now it didn't matter. The anticipation by now from all five of us was hardly bearable. We were so close, all of us looking around at each other with the tickets in our hands, we were still wondering what could go wrong and had to keep reminding each other that, no matter how we tried, we couldn't think of a thing. We watched the white cliffs of Dover get bigger and bigger, still not quite believing that we were there. As we drove off the ferry it all became real, nothing had stopped us. They dropped us off at Euston station in London and we made a call to home to tell them we had arrived. After all that we had made it. Against all the odds, the worries of being in Kabul with only a few pounds in our pockets was over. It was a strange feeling being back. After the build-up to our arrival, there seemed like something was missing. The anxiousness that we had felt for weeks that feeling we would not admit to ourselves, had gone, it was almost as if our life purpose was gone away and we were left with no feelings at all. Chris says, "I told you I'd get us back." Ugh!

We hardly spoke to each other on the train until we were back in Poulton still feeling a little empty but glad to be back with our families. It wasn't until we were back among our friends and telling the stories of what happened that the magnitude of what we had done sunk in. Most people at first didn't believe us but we knew it had all happened, all the stories as ridiculous as they may seem in good and bad fortune were as real as the games of cards and snooker played while we were away. Those stories had been our reality, so fantastic that friends back home though we were just making it up to make it and us sound good. Ridiculous as they may seem, you couldn't have made them up. I must admit, the other reality was, Chris was definitely more ridiculous than me, I swear it.

-oo-

Within a few weeks of being back, I had a job working for a big stationery company selling paper and kiddie's games. It was a good job but extremely pedestrian compared to what we had just been up to. Chris worked for a car paints company, then as a salesman in a lingerie company. He used to tell people he travelled in ladies underwear which always had folks in stitches.

170

From then we both were involved in many different things. Through the job, I moved to London temporarily staying in a hotel. I called Anne as she had given me her number and went to see her on a couple of occasions. She and Bob had split when they arrived back. Christine raised the cash to bail out her man to bring him back from being held in Afghanistan. Anne had an inheritance and was about to buy an antique shop in Kent so life was good for her.

Through my job, I met a girl and moved permanently to London and became involved firstly in computing, then the publicity and advertising business and many other things. Life was different for us and certainly none the worse for having made the trip. One downside for having the experience was that some things we did after took a lot of concentration not to be distracted by suddenly imagining we were back there but all the flashbacks, albeit some harrowing, were healthily character forming and we had gone through them. Others were sometimes too hilarious to relate if the folk you were talking to hadn't experienced the same or similar things.

-oo-

Living in Highgate in North London, I had made a plan to go to Poulton for the weekend and called Chris to arrange to go for a beer. He said that evening he was going out to dinner with his family and I should join them as he had something to tell me. He had stalls on markets selling all manner of trendy things for the last 15 years or so. Still the happy go lucky guy that couldn't navigate his way to the front garden, how he managed without me is still a mystery. He used to say the same thing about me which, in the company of people who knew him, used to bring the house down.

We all went to dinner and he started to tell me about the things he is selling, mugs with your name on them, leather wallets, sculptured candles and the like. There was a great demand for moccasin slippers which he was having a terrible time in sourcing. They were so popular that all the factories making them had sold their production for months, if not years ahead. Eventually, through a friend, he was given the number of a manufacturer that might have some spared him some stock.

Chris called him and arranged a meeting in a place at his factory in Blackburn. It was a miracle he found the place of course, without ending up in Brighton, but somehow he did.

The guy was friendly and because of his introduction, they got along fine and after some negotiation they agreed on a price for 5000 pairs. They had a beer and stayed to chat about this and that, Chris thinking if he kept the guy sweet, that he may give him some more as this batch would last no time at all. As they were chatting, in passing Chris told him of the trip to Australia and that we had come back overland, he had the guy fascinated for a while and they parted agreeing to meet tomorrow. Chris went back the next day to pay in advance for them to be delivered in a fortnight. When he turned up in the office they guy took the cash and asked him how his mate Stan was. Although they chatted the day before, he had not mentioned my name at all. He asked the guy how he knew. He then related back to Chris the details of our trip and how we got from Afghanistan all the way back to the UK, details that had not mentioned the day before. He said that on the way back in Afghanistan we had met two girls, Anne and Christine and one guy called Bob.

Chris by now had his mouth open and chin on the ground, the hairs on the back of his neck standing on end. The detail was so graphic and spine-chillingly accurate, for one of the first times in his life Chris was speechless. He thought the guy was some sort of medium or fortune teller or God was going to walk in the office (secretly he hoped, if there were a God, he would also turn up with another 5000 pairs of slippers). He continued by saying that the three were on the way back to England to raise money as their friend was held captive waiting for a ransom to be paid. Eventually, Chris beside himself and to avoid any wild imaginings or being any more astounded asked, "How the hell would you know all that?"

The guy said, "Well my friend, I have been waiting years to meet you and thank you for helping those people back to England. You and your friend were a tonic that they will never forget. You helped them out of their depression due to unfortunate circumstances with your jokes and quips and light-hearted approach to life." Chris was reeling with anticipation, no idea as to where all this was going.

"I thought you might have got it from the name, you see Chris, difficult as it may seem to believe, I was the guy James held in Afghanistan!"

-oo-